AF207231

I've Passed This Way Before

by Mike Coney

I've Passed This Way Before

Published by: Royal Coachman Publishing
15965 Fendt Farm Drive
Holland, MI 49424

Cover: by Matt Ryzenga

ISBN: 0-9678277-0-1

Library of Congress Catalog Card Number: 99-98251

Printed in the United States by
Morris Publishing
3212 East Highway 30
Kearney, NE 68847
1-800-650-7888

Dedication

To Laurie, my life's inspiration:
I can never thank you enough for being there. Your letters,
prayers, and thoughts enabled me to go on through many difficult
times. The little 'short time' calendar we sent back and forth across
the ocean so many times showed me how close I was to coming home
to you. Words can never express my feelings for you.

Thank-You

I would like to thank all of you who participated in the telling of my story. Thank-you, Tammy Barense and Cindy (Bink) Koedoot, for giving me the gentle push to get me started on something I knew I had to do, but couldn't start on my own.

Thank-you, Chris Linderman, Lyndsey Coney, and Bink, for all your hours of typing. At the ten-words-a-minute speed that I type, this book would never have been completed.

Thank you, Tammy and Bink for all the time spent correcting and editing.

Thank you all for your help, patience, and expertise.

Table of Contents

Prologue

As I sit here preparing to write a book, I ask myself, "Why would anyone want to read my story"? After all, many stories have been written about the Vietnam experience, by greater people than myself.

That may be the explanation I've been looking for--- experience. The Viet Nam War, along with that whole time period in history, was so complicated that it should be explained from every angle, and from many different sources.

I will not try to persuade anyone that one side or the other was right. I will leave politics, both the United State's and Vietnam's, out of my story. I just want to tell the reader about my year. I wish to explain it in a way that will not offend young or old, male or female.

I'm proud of my service to my country, and I'm proud of the guys with whom I served. I have many regrets, but I will not use this book to express them. I want to share experiences that are interesting and funny, as well as heart-breaking.

It has taken me twenty-seven years, without a day going by that I don't think about Vietnam, to write this book. Smells, noises, birds, voices, temperature, darkness, rain, and many other everyday occurrences can send me back there, instantly. It may be difficult for others to understand how any experience can occupy most of your waking and sleeping hours, but that is why I feel I should share my year.

APO 96225

A young man once went off to war
in a far country
When he had time, he wrote home and
said, " Sure rains here a lot."

But his mother, reading between the lines,
Wrote, " We're quite concerned. Tell us
what it's really like."

And the young man responded, " Wow, you ought
to see the funny monkeys!"

To which his mother replied, " Don't
hold back, how is it?"

And the young man wrote, "The sunsets here
are spectacular."

In her next letter the mother
wrote, "Son we want you to tell us
everything."

So the next time he wrote,
"Today I killed a man.
Yesterday I helped drop napalm on women and
children. Tomorrow we are going to use
gas."

And the father wrote, " Please don't write
such depressing letters. You're upsetting
your mother."

So, after a while, the young man wrote, "Sure rains a
lot here..."

Larry Rottmann, U.S. Army

April, 1967

My year unofficially started in Okinawa. We were making a refueling stop at Kadena Air Force Base, Okinawa. We were told we could stretch our legs for an hour, before continuing on to Vietnam. After fifteen hours of flight from San Francisco, all 325 of us poured out of the plane laughing, joking, and pushing, just like kids at recess. The next stop would be different; never again would we be kids.

I decided to make a phone call to my hometown buddy who was in the Marines. He had been injured in Okinawa and was in the hospital. I found out he had just been discharged from the hospital so I tried the Marine base. While the operator tried to connect us at his base, I looked out the pay phone windows and casually watched jet fighters and B-52's continually taking off. As his sergeant told me they couldn't find him, I got this funny sinking feeling in my stomach. Realization had hit; those planes and I were going to war.

I was a nineteen-year-old, naive kid from Holland, Michigan. I had volunteered to go to Vietnam, because it seemed like the right thing to do. I had always been adventurous. I had nothing else to do; my dad was a World War II vet, and I had seen all the John Wayne movies. I had at least a million "good" reasons to volunteer. God, how stupid I was!

1

After boarding the plane, I listened to two soldiers in the next seat brag about how many V.C. they would kill. To tell the truth, I hadn't given that much thought. Here I was on a plane headed to a war zone and hadn't thought much about killing or survival. I was just sure I would survive.

I was shaken from my thoughts as the plane banked to the right for our approach to Ton Son Nhut Air Base. My first sight of Vietnam was the patchwork layout of rice paddies. It was no longer a funny feeling in my stomach---it was fear. You could have heard a pin drop; the plane was so quiet. As the plane taxied to a halt, the stewardess wished us luck over the intercom and opened the door. As I filed out she said, "See you next year." I was about to say "Count on it," when the heat hit me like a sledgehammer--- followed closely by the strangest smell. A soldier at the bottom of the stairs said, "Grab your duffel bag and walk to the shelter." It couldn't have been more than 200 yards, but I thought I would pass out from the heat. My uniform was soaked with sweat. My shoes stuck to the tar. It had to be 115° and extremely humid. I felt almost claustrophobic from the heat. The smell of hot rotting vegetation mixed with diesel fuel turned my stomach.

We were transported from the airport to Long Binh Base Camp by a bus. The bus had chicken wire over the windows to keep hand grenades from being thrown inside. This was Lesson One of my real education. I was beginning an education to which I would pay close attention. If only my teachers in school could have gotten my attention like this, maybe I wouldn't be here. I wanted Lesson Two; I needed it.

In my wildest imagination I couldn't have pictured this. It was a city in constant motion. The sights, sounds, and smells were overpowering and ever present. There was no escape from

2

them. There seemed to be a constant swirl of movement. People were everywhere---all so close, and all talking at the same time. Bicycles, motorcycles, cars and military vehicles of every description were weaving in and out amongst each other at a slow pace. Who was the enemy; the dreaded Viet Cong we had been told about? Lesson Two: He and she are everywhere---waiting and watching for an opportunity.

It was all so confusing; I felt like I had fallen off the world into this confusing place. To top it all off, a civilian bus in front of us had stopped, which stopped us. Because of the oncoming, non-stop traffic and narrow road, we were forced to wait until it moved. Everyone on the civilian bus got off and went to the bathroom, right there in broad daylight - in front of everyone else! This confirmed it, I had dropped off the real world into this strange, exotic place. Lesson Three: Forget modesty. In fact, chuck everything you ever thought was normal.

We eventually made it to Long Binh Base Camp. This was one of many dispersal points for all personnel coming in or leaving Vietnam. We were told we would have to pull guard duty if we were still there the next night. Our only instructions were to drink lots of water and to get in a bunker if we were attacked. Before night fall, I left our temporary quarters to try and catch a breeze. I found out there isn't such a thing as fresh air in Vietnam.

I was leaning against a sandbag wall when a black guy came over and asked for a light. He leaned against the wall and stared off into the evening, enjoying his smoke. As we talked about the heat, I couldn't help but notice how undernourished he looked, but more than that was the look in his eyes. They had a far away, dead look to them. Vets have a term for this. It's called the thousand yard stare. I asked him where he was headed. He proceeded to tell me he was returning from Japan and was avoiding returning to his unit. He said he had been wounded twice and he was scared to return. Now, I'm not overly superstitious, but I felt like taking a step back, out of the line of fire. I didn't know what to say. I couldn't wish him good luck; he had none. If I felt this way, a know-nothing new guy, how would his buddies feel to see him return? As I walked away from him, his cigarette glowing in the dark, I wondered what would happen to him. I knew I would probably never have that question answered. This was the beginning of a year of many unanswered questions, still unanswered questions.

That night I tossed and turned in my rack, suffering from the heat. My last duty station was Alaska. When I left, it was minus 50 degrees. Michigan was in the thirties. I really thought I would suffocate from the heat. I thought that, until I heard machine gun and small arms fire on the perimeter.

Suffocation---gone, replaced by the thought of being killed on my first night in the country. Where was the bunker?--- think! Lesson Four: Never, ever go anywhere without knowing the location and exits to safety. Bunkers would become a way of life for the next year.

I must have stubbed my toes on everything in that building. Do I stop to put boots and clothing on? The firing intensified, giving me the answer to that question. By the time I reached the bunker, it was all over. Whatever happened was over. Time to go back to sleep---right! I laid on my bunk with my clothes on and prayed for the sun. Welcome to Vietnam!

On Day Two in-country, I learned two things. The first was that I was assigned to the 25th Military Police, 25th Infantry Division in a place called Cu Chi. The second thing I learned was how important the days gone by in-country would be. Every conversation started with, "How short are you?" Anyone hearing about my 364 days (it was leap year) and counting, would laugh, tease, and proudly explain how many days they had left. Very seldom was there pity. Everyone else was so short they had to untie their shoestrings to see.

I was joined by ten other guys for the convoy trip to Cu Chi. I had no idea what to expect and neither did anyone else. We climbed into the back of a deuce and a half truck, which held M-16's and ammunition magazines for everyone. We locked and loaded our 16's and, as usual in the army, we waited. About mid-afternoon the convoy moved out. The convoy was made up of hundreds of military vehicles all in line, rolling down the highway. Little did I know that I would soon be providing protection for these daily convoys.

The transformation from city to country was amazing and quick. Everything was moving too fast, especially the convoy. Everybody and everything got out of the way. All civilian traffic, whether a cart, bus or lambretta, got off the road. We didn't stop once in the two hour trip.

I was trying to absorb everything. My eyes and mind just couldn't keep up. The trip was just like landing at Ton Son Nhut; no one spoke. I tried to take in all of the sights: rice paddies, modes of transportation, strange animals and birds, people in all stages of dress and work, jungle, Buddhist Temples, and monkeys. If only I had my camera. It was buried inside my duffel bag. I'm sure my parents and my girlfriend, Laurie, would appreciate seeing some of this. If I lay this rifle down... wait a minute what about Lesson Two: The enemy is everywhere. I'm not on vacation here. They gave me this rifle for a purpose. In all I observed over those miles, I never once thought about looking for the enemy. What does he or she look like? For what am I supposed to be looking? I felt like an idiot. We soon turned off the main road in the center of the little village of Cu Chi and headed north toward the sprawling base camp of the 25th Infantry Division. Approximately a half mile before the gate, we passed through a complex array of open fronted stores. All the horns on the trucks started blasting. I was soon to find out this was Tropic Lightning Road. I couldn't help noticing all the Vietnamese girls, and no men other than bands of GI's roaming the street. It didn't take a genius to figure out what was going on here. I'd have a better picture of Tropic Lightning Road soon.

As we passed through the guarded gate of the base camp, monsoon rains started up. It rained harder than I'd ever seen it rain. I took this as an omen. Like I've said, I'm not overly superstitious, but this didn't look good. Entering my new home, drenched to the bone, things couldn't get worse I thought. I was wrong.

My next few days were spent adjusting to the heat at a transient center. I filled sand bags and drank water all day. This entire country should be under water from the filling of sandbags. Everywhere you looked there were sandbags - sandbag walls surrounding buildings, sandbag bunkers in which to hide, sandbag walkways, and that was just in the center of one base camp. The bunker line surrounding the base must have had millions of sandbags in it. Someone was making a fortune selling sandbags.

I found out that the base camp was about one mile wide and three or four miles long. There were about 20,000 soldiers that called Cu Chi home, but there were seldom that many on the base camp at one time. Thousands at a time were out in the boonies on operations. The base camp was just a center of operations for us. To the enemy, it was a big target. Keep filling those sandbags!

I reported to my company area early in the morning and was shown to my bunk. My hootch was shared with thirteen other guys I was soon to meet. There were ten hootches on each side of a street. All the hootches were raised off the ground about two feet to keep them as dry and cool as possible. My hootch had a tin roof. The hootches on the other side of the street were thatched.

I put all of my equipment in a trunk, and was ordered by a sergeant to help with the construction of a new bunker. Three other guys were already digging a ten foot by ten foot hole. I was introduced to Norman from Oklahoma, Boone from California and Simari from New York.

I'm pretty quiet, which tends to make people want to tell me things. Besides, I'm a firm believer in: you listen, you learn.

During that day, I learned a lot and made three new friends. During eight hours of digging, I learned the following:

-You have to rely on people, but you have to be careful where you place your trust. You must learn which officers and NCO's to trust. You have to trust your squad members.

-You cannot trust any Vietnamese. You can work with them, play with them and like them, but don't put your trust in them.

-Monsoon season was just starting. (Is that why we're digging in the rain?)

-Malaria pills are a must. Expect the worst cramps and runs of your life.

-Your weapon must be clean at all times. (M-16's are notorious for jamming.)

-The beans and franks C-rations are the best. The ham and lima beans are the worst.

-If you can, take your shower in the afternoon when there is still water, and it's also hot from the afternoon sun.

-Do not touch anything that crawls or slithers.

-Wherever you go, know where the bunkers are. (Knew that one already!)

-Do not eat anything the Vietnamese give you, unless they eat some of it first.

-If the kids disappear, you know trouble is coming.

-Do not go near water buffaloes. (They hate the smell of Americans.)

All in all, it was a very useful couple of days. Not only did we build a bunker that could probably survive a direct hit, but also I learned a lot.

For the next few weeks, I was placed on General's Guard. I worked four hours on, four hours off, as a bodyguard. It sounds more exciting than it was. For the most part, I would walk around General Wyend's or General Gleason's hootch the entire shift. I was supposed to wake them when we received incoming rounds, and watch for enemy sappers.

The first night we were mortared, I learned that the General's Guard was also a reaction force. I was told this as I was sitting in the safety of our newly constructed bunker, after a mad dash from a sound sleep. Norman said from a dark corner of the bunker, "You're supposed to surround the command bunker and protect it from a ground attack." My first reaction was, "You can't be serious. I'm suppose to sprint across one hundred yards of open field during a mortar attack, just to sit out in the open? Why on earth did I put so much sweat into the building of this bunker?" Everybody in the bunker said they didn't know, but they sure appreciated the effort.

On another hot night a week later, I heard the now familiar sound of mortars dropping on the base camp. It was the first time it happened while I was on duty. I could hear the rounds walking up the base camp in my direction. I rushed in on the sleeping general. I'm sure I was shouting, especially as the shells got closer, "General, wake up, incoming shells." I then went back outside to guard the door. The shells were close enough to see the bright flashes. If I wasn't shouting before, I was now, "Move out, General!" I hugged the protective wall surrounding his hootch, and I prayed for him to hurry. I rushed back in to find, to my amazement, that he had gone out another door, to the safety of the command bunker. I made a mad dash for the bunker also, cursing him the entire distance. By the time I reached the door, the attack was over. Our choppers were up, and the V.C. were disappearing, almost as fast as my general.

My mom didn't raise a fool, and my girlfriend wasn't waiting for a coffin to come home, so I applied, and was granted a transfer to regular M.P. duty. The guys in my hootch couldn't believe I wanted to get off the gravy job of General's Guard for their duty. That didn't sound good. Oh well, too late now; move on.

May, June, and July; 1967

I transferred to regular M.P. duty which entailed learning many new and interesting assignments. Each assignment was usually one week long.

The assignments were:
1. Convoy Security
2. Gate Guard
3. Dump Guard (That's right!)
4. Tropic Lightning Road Patrol
5. Hoc Mon Bridge Guard
6. Post Patrol

Convoy Security had to be the closest thing to being a cowboy as I could imagine. It was exciting, plain and simple. From the second I got up and dressed, I was pumped up. I wasn't sure what to expect, but I thought I was ready.

I was teamed with two other guys. Bill Carson, from Ohio, would be the driver of the jeep. Rayfield Scott, called Scotty, from Detroit, would be shot gunner and radio operator. I was the machine gunner. The weapon was an M-60 machine gun mounted on a post in the back of the jeep. I could stand up or sit on the spare tire. Either way, I had to hang on for dear life. Besides the M-60, we all had M-16's, and our sidearms which were .45 caliber pistols. We wore flak jackets and steel pots at all times.

Scotty didn't talk much, probably because Bill talked constantly. Since I'm pretty much a listener, Bill would become my best friend. He explained Convoy Security like this: Every morning we meet the empty trucks in the marshaling area outside of Cu Chi. While they're put in position for the run to Saigon, we provide security. Watch everyone and everything. Two machine gun jeeps will take the front, two spread out in the convoy, and two at the rear. We will rotate positions when the need arises. If there is a problem, or just as a precaution, the two lead jeeps will pull off and provide cover as the convoy rolls past. The other jeeps will hop, skip, and jump into the vacated positions. The two covering jeeps will then fall in behind the convoy. We operate at full speed and never stop. We take up both lanes of traffic, so we can rotate through the convoy. All civilian traffic pulls off the road. The only place we slow down is at Hoc Mon Bridge. The original bridge was blown up and replaced with a temporary army bridge. We have military police and ARVN's guarding the bridge against attack during our crossing.

The machine gun jeeps are in constant radio contact with each other, Hoc Mon Bridge, and a helicopter. The helicopter has an officer in charge of the convoy and warns us of possible problems. His call sign was "Sheriff." The trucks do not have radios, so we signal them with hand gestures.

Since the trucks are empty, the V.C. usually leave us alone on the trip to Saigon. We just get the convoy to Saigon, and then we return to Cu Chi, picking up the guards at Hoc Mon as we go by. Another unit from Saigon will make the return trip to Cu Chi the next afternoon. That resupply convoy will be loaded with everything from Coca-Cola to ammunition.

Sounds simple enough, I thought. I temporarily forgot Lesson Two and Three: The V.C. are everywhere, and nothing is normal in Vietnam.

We had cleared the marshaling area at the crack of dawn, no ambushes or mines. The first trucks were rolling in, when Sheriff One radioed us. "Check out possible enemy movement three miles south of Cu Chi on Highway One. Keep in radio contact. Sheriff One, out."

We all had adrenalin flowing as we sped through Cu Chi. At the designated spot, Sheriff One told us to stop and look around. The spot was a long, straight stretch of Highway One, with rice paddies on either side. Approximately two hundred yards beyond the paddies, jungle began. Farmers were plowing the family plots with their water buffaloes. All was quiet, almost serene. After thirty minutes of waiting, I decided to take a picture of this peaceful scene. I took one picture from the road and decided I needed a better angle. I climbed up on the back bench of the jeep---perfect. I found the farmer in my little instamatic lens, and was adjusting to fit the water buffalo in, when I heard this angry, buzzing bee sound followed by a cracking sound. Still standing there, I looked at my buddies and said, "What was that?"

From their prone position behind the jeep they said, "Sniper! Get your ass down!" I didn't feel scared. More than anything, I felt angry and shocked, both at the enemy and at myself. How stupid I "Joe Target" was, standing up in the back of the jeep taking pictures. Charlie probably missed because he was giggling. Which brings me to him. He doesn't even know me, and he wants to kill me! The more I thought about it, the angrier I got. As we were speeding away, I tried to put things into perspective. First and foremost, the camera got put away.

Secondly, do not get angry; do not take this personally. This is survival of the fittest. (Today was survival of the luckiest.) Think, think, think, every second, think. Fortunately, I still have a brain between my ears, but only because of a few inches mistake in elevation, or giggling. Charlie, you faceless enemy, you taught me many valuable lessons today. You won't ever have it so easy again. We drove away without firing a shot; that won't ever happen again either. I had over one thousand rounds of ammo in the jeep, and more where that came from.

When we reported back to Sheriff One, we explained how we would spray the area as the convoy rolled past. He said his chopper would also hose down the jungle.

"Head 'em up and roll 'em out," Sheriff One ordered and off we went. We took point, because we knew where he "was". At the spot, which will remain etched in my memory forever, we pulled to the side of the road. I fired short bursts from my machine gun for ten minutes as the convoy rolled past. I don't know if there was any return fire or not because of all the noise from the trucks, but I felt better.

We pulled in behind the last truck, firing as we hit top speed. One oddity in this whole sequence, from beginning to end, stuck in my mind. As the enemy fired and we fired back, the farmer continued plowing his rice paddy. The road is raised about ten feet, so we were firing right over his head into the jungle. He kept right on plowing as if he'd seen this happen before, probably many times. Maybe the first time it happened, he had also decided not to take this personally. Either life goes on, or it doesn't.

The rest of the day was uneventful in the sense that we didn't get shot at. The convoy made it safely to Saigon and began preparing for the return trip the next day. We, on the other hand, did some quick shopping at the PX on Tan Son Nuet Air Base. We all had our lists of needed supplies from people in CuChi. The whole time I was picking things up, I couldn't help notice how people stared at us. I knew we were dust covered, dirty, and sweaty, but they looked at us like we were from outer space. Then it hit me; it was all the weapons we carried. I was astonished. Not one single person on the base had a weapon. I asked Bill what the story was. He said it was against the law for them to carry weapons. There were weapons somewhere, but they were locked up. Someday they would pay for this stupidity.

After leaving the PX, we waited at the gate for the proper time to pull out for our return trip. This time spent only enhanced our image of being cowboys. The military police at the gate weren't even allowed to load their pistols. We soon had a crowd gathered, inspecting our weapons and asking what it was like out there. I found that this was a lot like fishing. The stories got bigger and better with time. Most of these soldiers would spend their entire year on this base and never realize there was a war going on. Maybe they could catch it on T.V. over a good meal in their air-conditioned club. Slow down, cowboy, you're starting to sound jealous. Actually, I wasn't; I still found it exciting.

Bill said, "Let's lock and load. Time to hat up." A quiet settled over the crowd, as if someone had said it was high noon. Time to head down to the OK Corral. We put on our flak jackets and our steel pots, and of course, chambered a round into our weapons. Naturally, we did this with flourish and style. There were some very sincere,"Good lucks," and off we went into the sunset. (Actually, the sun wouldn't set for another two hours but it seemed fitting.) It was now time to shake off the bravado and start thinking. Six machine gun jeeps were flying down Highway One as fast as possible. About two miles from Hoc Mon Bridge we radioed the M.P.s there to "Crank 'em up". As we passed them, their jeeps fell in behind us. The sun was starting to set, and no one wanted to be out after dark. Just outside of Cu Chi, we radioed ahead that we'd be at the gate in five minutes. We rolled through the gate to safety, just as it was getting dark. Safe and sound, but not yet finished. The jeeps had to be gassed, and our weapons cleaned before we could get cleaned up and eat.

By the time I had written a letter to Laurie, I was bushed. Before the electricity went off, I read through the letter. The events in the letter were different than what actually happened, but no sense in making everyone worried back home.

As I lay in my rack before falling asleep, I promised myself I would write Laurie everyday, and I would not make her worry. I'll keep my problems to myself, and maybe some day write a book. Those two promises would be hard to keep. I would write everyday, but it would become hard not to share what was going on in my life.

Dawn was upon us all too quickly. It found us in almost the same spot as yesterday. It wasn't the same spot, because you could never do the same thing twice in a row in Vietnam. Someone was always watching, waiting for a mistake.

We were approximately five miles out of Cu Chi when Sheriff One radioed us that the lead jeep had been ambushed and was disabled. Everyone was out of the jeep and the convoy was still rolling. He wanted to make sure that the vehicle was completely destroyed.

My dilemma was, could I put two hand grenades at once

into the jeep? Thinking safety, I opted for one grenade. I scored a direct hit. The explosion set off the gas tank and the five gallon gas can on the back of the jeep. Sheriff One radioed that not much could be stripped off what was left. We were all anxious to get to Tan Son Nuet to hear what happened. The stories would be interesting today. As it turned out, the three guys didn't know what happened. They assumed it was one person with an AK-47. He put twenty rounds or more into the jeep, hoping to stop the convoy. He blew out the windows, radiator and all the tires, but did not touch anyone. It was a miracle; they managed to get it off the road and jumped into the next jeep without suffering a scratch. Scratch one jeep, but that can be replaced. They even managed to take all of their weapons with them.

The return trip was quiet, as were the next two days. The lull in action allowed me to think about spots I would set up an ambush if I were Viet Cong. The lull in activity also allowed us to practice shooting while standing in an open jeep moving at about fifty miles per hour. There *was* a road sign just outside of Hoc Mon, with the face of a man brushing his teeth. I say, *was*, because we removed his face with machine gun fire. If only my dad could see his tax dollars at work.

One spot on Highway One, near Saigon, always made the hair on the back of my neck stand up. The road narrowed down due to buildings coming up to the edge of the road on one side, and rubber trees, all in rows, coming up to the edge on the other side. The trees should have been cut back for security reasons. The reason they weren't, I was told, was that the U.S. army would have to pay the owner of the rubber plantation $200 for each tree taken down. Maybe if we didn't use so much ammo on the signs we could afford to cut down the trees.

On the fifth day of Convoy Duty, my worst fears came true. We had been in and out of monsoon rains all day. This made me wonder, "How could it be pouring down rain on one side of the road and the sun be shining on the opposite lane?" The rain was so on and off that we didn't bother putting our ponchos on. As fast as we were moving, a raincoat wouldn't do much good anyway.

We were riding point, almost to Saigon, and my thoughts turned to a water buffalo burger and French fries on Tan Son Nuet. As I tilted my head against the driving rain, I could pick out the shapes of the rubber trees approaching. The hair on the back of my neck stood up. We were approaching one of the spots I thought was an excellent place to spring an ambush. As we got to the tree line, we burst out of the rain. As a precaution, I swung the M-60 toward the trees. At the same time, I heard a loud crack, and I knew the jeep behind us had been hit. My eyes focused on a small circle of smoke hanging in the still air, targeting the spot from where I assumed the shot came. I pumped quite a few rounds into that circle of smoke, knowing Charlie had to be somewhere behind it, in the top of the tree. As we pulled off to let the convoy go by, I noticed something drop from the tree. Sheriff One wanted to know what was going on, so we explained the situation. We were all surprised when he told us to investigate further and keep him informed. Six of us spread out and moved forward from tree to tree. I was shaking like a leaf, and the adrenalin was being pushed by the gallon. Slow down, think. Were we being lured into a bigger ambush? Except for my heart beating in my throat, it was so quiet. I could see a rifle laying on the ground. It was a Chinese SKS semi-automatic weapon. My gaze went up the tree to a camouflaged body. He was tied to the tree, and no one was going up after him. Sheriff One solved the problem for us, "Leave him as a warning to others. Take the weapon and catch up to the convoy. Sheriff One, out." Bill said, "You heard him. Let's get out of here."

That body stayed there until there was nothing left but bones, but we were never hit from that spot again.

Our problems weren't over for the day. On our return trip, Bill hit a big pig as we passed through a hamlet. The pig ran out in front of us, and he couldn't avoid it. Almost in slow motion, the jeep turned on its side. I came out of it the best, because I was standing up. My flak jacket absorbed a lot of the shock of hitting the road. I rolled and stood up. Bill and Scotty had a few abrasions, but, all in all, we were pretty lucky. The villagers helped us right the jeep and then we had to negotiate with the farmer for his pay. Since it was getting dark, he got a pretty good deal, plus he got to keep the pig. We gave him 1000 piasters (about $10.00), and we were on our way.

The rest of my time on Convoy Security was uneventful, although interesting, and a new learning experience everyday. With each passing day, I knew I was learning things that would keep me alive. I was also getting short!

When Convoy Security ended, I have to admit I was relieved. Of all the assignments we had, it was the most dangerous. Not only was it dangerous, but also the wear and tear on your body was excruciating. Weather conditions, four hours of sleep a night, and constantly paying attention to every detail begins to take its toll. Gate Guard Duty was next in our line of rotation.

Gate Guard was very boring and lasted all night. Just you and the mosquitoes.

There were three gates into the base camp. The Ann Margret Gate was never used, except for operations that went off into the jungle. Ambush Gate was the entry and exit for all convoys. The Main Gate led to Tropic Lighting Road and Cu Chi.

Three events stand out during my fourteen days on Guard Duty. My first night on Ambush Gate, I arrived on duty about 6 p.m. The guard shack was on posts, a square three feet by three feet, with a slanted tin roof, and surrounded by the ever-present sandbags. Monsoon season was gaining strength so most of the night I was a tired, sodden lump of mosquito bites.

There is no gate at Ambush Gate. Actually, it's more of a break in the defensive perimeter, with a road. At night, a truck mounted Quad Fifty is rolled into the gap in the line.

My purpose in being there would be, umm, good question. Let me think about it. After all, I had all night. If I were the Viet Cong, and I wanted to breach the perimeter, would I attack the fortified, mine field laden bunker line, full of soldiers in waiting? Or would I send a rocket straight down the road into the truck parked there, and then pour through the breach? Ah, there was my purpose. I was the final line of defense against the communist horde. As I tightened my flack jacket down, secured my steel pot, and also distanced myself from the truck, I heard a noise.

Night in Vietnam was the darkest place on earth. There were no lights anywhere, and because of the monsoon season the moon and stars were hidden by clouds. There were some people that actually got claustrophobic because of the dark.

My finger tightened down on the safety of my M-16. Do I whisper to the gunner in the turret of the Quad Fifty? If I heard

it, he must have heard it. Wait a minute, that noise was coming
from my left side, not out in front. "Psst," came out of the
darkness.

"Be wide awake. There are V.C. out there."

"No bull," I said. "This is Vietnam, you know."

"What I mean, is we've seen them with a starlight."

I walked toward his voice and asked if I could have a
look. We entered the bunker and approached the gun port. I
could hear everyone's excited whispers. One guy was on the
radio, trying to get permission from the duty officer to open fire.

I looked into the eye piece and immediately saw
movement. There was the communist horde, well, eight of them
anyway. I couldn't believe my eyes, black pajamas, AK-47's,
and they were crawling across the road, not fifty yards in front
of my post. Yipes, I'd better get back and warn everyone else.

I ran out of the bunker and back to my post, as quietly as
possible. The quad fifty gunner sat in a turret on top of a flat
bed deuce and a half truck. Thinking about the possibility of a
rocket flying down the road, I tried to whisper to this guy. No
reaction. I would have to climb up onto this target. In the dark,
I couldn't tell what was what. Funny, it was so clear when it
was sunny and safe. All I could feel was plastic. The gunner
had draped his poncho over the gun barrels and was fast asleep.
After finding him and shaking him awake, I explained what was
happening. As I was talking, I could hear the noise of an
approaching jeep. Great, it's the night duty officer and his
driver checking up on me. What else can go wrong? I jumped
off the truck, misjudged the height and tumbled to the ground. It
seemed like enough noise to wake everyone in the entire country.
Why didn't I just put a glowing target on myself and get it over
with? The jeep had two glowing dots on it that acted

as headlights so they could see the road. I circled out of the lights-- trying to save my night vision. I approached the jeep at a crawl. The sergeant heard me, but couldn't see, and in a loud voice said, "Do you know the duty officer is in this jeep, soldier?"

"Yes I do, and now, so does every Charlie in the vicinity," I whispered.

After I once again explained the situation, they put the jeep in reverse, disappearing in a hurry. I couldn't help but laugh. The sergeant was talking in the direction of where my head would normally have been, but I was on the ground. Little things just may keep me alive for the next ten months.

I asked the gunner if anything new had happened, but there was no answer. I went back up on the truck to shake him awake. He didn't remember me waking him the first time. Little things may get me killed also.

Finally, I could settle down in the protection of my little guard shack and wait for the firing to start.

I waited, wide eyed, until dawn without a single shot being fired. With the sun, usually comes safety. Feeling safe, I walked over to the bunker where this all began. " What happened?" I asked. "Apparently there was an American ambush patrol out there, and they were afraid they would get caught in the crossfire," said one of the sleepy bunker guards. Another frustrating night in Vietnam. Probably, quite a few more to go. In fact, within two days I'd have another one.

This time it took place at Main Gate. My purpose here was about the same as Ambush Gate with one added assignment. I had to count each individual soldier leaving the base camp on Ambush Patrol, and then count them again when they returned. The V.C. have been known to tag on, in the dark, to the returning line of soldiers. Once on the base camp, they create chaos by blowing up choppers, fuel, ammo dumps, and other strategic targets. This strategy also gets nervous American soldiers firing at each other out of fear. Good discipline can prevent this, but occasionally, discipline gives into fear.

I came on duty at about 6:00 p.m. I relieved the three guards on duty. There were three because they are much busier during the day. After six, no one, except Ambush Patrols, enters or leaves base camp. This was my favorite time of day. It was starting to cool off, and the base camp was quieting down. If it's not raining, the sun sets are the most beautiful in the world. You can hear the birds and frogs like no where else. I was enjoying the peaceful scene, because I knew that once the sunset was gone, all peace and serenity disappeared. Thinking this, I reached for my helmet and flak jacket.

My thoughts were interrupted by an approaching lambretta, a three wheeled mini bus powered by a motorcycle engine that can hold about eight tightly packed people. They were all over the roads, but never approached the base camp. I didn't like the looks of this, so I locked and loaded my M-16. At Main Gate they usually clogged the entrance with a tank, but it wasn't in position yet. I whistled at the tank crew lounging on the tank parked down the street. "Heads up, something's going to happen," I said.

I had heard other G.I.'s talk about suicide attacks, but I couldn't imagine a Lambretta being used for one. The little bus stopped at the guard shack, knowing it would be suicide to go any further. The driver jumped out and very excitedly motioned me to the back of the mini-bus. The only words I could make out were bac si and moulin, which mean "doctor" and "hurry". I peeked into the back of the bus with my rifle

22

raised. My gaze was met by the gaze of a very old lady that had very little time left on this earth. Through hand gestures, and the little Vietnamese I knew, I found out she had been gored by a water buffalo. The huge animal had ripped her from below her belly button to the middle of her chest. From all the leaves and dirt in the wound, I knew they had tried to replace her intestines.

Normal procedure any other place in the world would be to rush them to the hospital, but this wasn't normal and it was definitely not like any other place in the world.

I couldn't let them go. I had to frisk them, search under their vehicle, and worst of all, make them lift her to see if she was booby trapped. The Viet Cong booby trapped everything.

I had already radioed for a post patrol jeep to escort them to the med-evac hospital. That left me the rest of the night to ponder what had just happened.

I knew I was no longer a "new guy." I was becoming a vet, suspicious of everyone and everything. In just a few months in-country my transition was amazing. From a kind, fun-loving kid, to a cold, calculating, callous, survivor of the fittest G.I.

Maybe I wasn't quite there yet, because through the night, I wondered and cared about what had happened to her. I probably would never know. I knew they wouldn't let her relatives leave during the night. It was against the law for any Vietnamese to be out after dark. Only the enemy moved at night, and anyone out after dark was subject to being fired upon. Simply going outside to go to the bathroom could cost a Vietnamese his life. Simple mistakes in this country were costly for all of us.

The sun marked the end of another night of Guard Duty. Safe again, and one day shorter. My route back to the company area took me past the med-evac. Through sleepy eyes, I saw a Lambretta being loaded with a body bag. I was right, another day had begun in Vietnam.

My last day of Guard Duty was exactly that, day light guard duty. I had been on Guard Duty until 6:00 a.m. and came back on duty at noon. Not having had enough sleep, I found myself staring down the road and into space. Staring at everything and nothing. As the heat of day hit full force, I took shelter in the guard shack and continued to stare down the road, now aided by binoculars. What caught my attention, and woke me up were the sounds of a farmer digging a well. He'd asked, and been given permission, to dig the well about a half mile from camp. What really made me pay attention was that he went into the hole without a shirt and came out with one on, and then, a short time later, emerged wearing a different colored one. After hours of watching, I said something to the duty officer. Shortly, we had fourteen soldiers surrounding the "well". When we peered over the wall, all we could see was water.

As a kid, I always enjoyed firecrackers, and now as a bigger kid, I enjoyed bigger explosives. I produced a hand grenade, of which I always had plenty. No one volunteered to go down the well, so down the grenade went. The result was amazing. Eighteen "farmers" suddenly came bobbing to the top. They had dug down to below water level, then dug over, and dug back up to just above the water line. Then, they had proceeded to dig toward the base camp. They hadn't gotten very far toward the base camp when my grenade ruined their train of thought and their hearing.

We turned the prisoners over to the guards at the prisoner of war stockade. The guards were American, and the interrogators were Vietnamese. The interrogators would separate the Viet Cong from the forced laborers. Anyway you looked at it, they were in for a long and painful night.

This wasn't the only tunnel we encountered. The V.C. were like moles, constantly digging. The Cu Chi area was honeycombed with miles and miles of tunnels. The way this war was run, we probably bought the dirt taken from the tunnels to fill our sandbags.

When you have lots of time, time that can't be spent talking to others, you end up doing some pretty heavy thinking. Often, I wondered how dedicated to a cause would you have to be to risk your life underground. I would have an answer to my question in a month.

My next assignment was Dump Duty, officially Sanitation Protective Services. I didn't know what it was, but it had to be easier than Convoy Security. For one thing, we didn't start until 8 a.m., and we were through at 4:30 p.m. or 1630 army time.

How hard could it be to guard a dump, and what is it we guard? I should have known, this is Vietnam, nothing is easy or normal.

The dump, as I found out, was a huge hole in the ground, about a half mile long, surrounded by concertina, or rolled barb wire. The dump was about one mile, or less, from the village of Van Cau. As I was to find out, the village survived on what it got from the dump, which was considerable. Twenty-five thousand G.I.'s produce, use, and discard a considerable amount of items each day.

A young guy named Castro and I had duty together. He had been doing this for several weeks, which told me he had gotten on the wrong side of someone's list. Along with us was a Vietnamese military policeman, called a Q.C. He was to act as our interpreter, even though he spoke no English. His one unique and usable feature was his ability to open Coke bottles with his teeth. I was totally amazed at this, until I found out the Coke girls pop the tops, pour half into another bottle, and add water. Double the product, for double the price. Because of the heat, we went through many, many bottles of Coke. We began to think Q.C.'s initials meant. "Quality Coke" opener.

Castro explained our assignment like this: "We drive to one side of the dump and chase people away, while hundreds of people pour into the other side of the dump. We turn around and do the same thing all day long. At 4:30, they set everything on fire and we're done."

Doubting his numbers I asked, "Why do they run if they outnumber us?"

"If they don't, the Q.C. will fire his tommy gun over their heads, and since he is so small, he loses control quite often. He's hit a few of them by accident," said Castro.

I guess our Q.C. had two unique features. Mental note, when I hear the rattle of his weapon, hit it. Better yet, know where he is at all times. There is nothing in this dump worth dying for, and I'm beginning to think its true for this entire country.

It didn't take me long to see the futility and stupidity of this assignment. Castro was right, there were literally hundreds of people waiting for the first trucks to arrive. Young and old, men, women and children were ready to start work. They all carried bags and wore some form of non-fitting boots and gloves, and a very determined look on their faces. As the trucks started dumping, they pointed to the areas they were claiming. They looked right through us as if we didn't count as an obstacle. I was to find out they were right. When they decided to begin, it was frightening how fast we lost control, if we'd ever had it. They were through the barbed wire in seconds, into the dump, and filling their bags. We began a chase which caused a few people to drop their bags. They seemed to have an endless supply of bags, so they weren't too concerned about that.

We spent the entire morning flying back and forth, accomplishing nothing. For every plan we came up with, they had a counter plan. They had been at this for quite a few years, so they had seen everything we tried. I was becoming angrier as the morning went along, almost to the point of being irrational. I was ready to turn our coke bottle opening, machine gun toting Q.C. loose. Like a rabid little ferret, he was ready. Fortunately, the post patrol jeep showed up to relieve us for lunch. It gave me the opportunity to calm down, gather my thoughts, and enjoy the peace and quiet. It was peaceful and quiet, because no one would sit with us in the mess hall. From now on, I would know who had dump guard also. We stunk!

On the way back to the dump, I had an idea. What could they get from this dump that would aide Charlie? Food was the item they got most of the time, and it was beginning to putrefy in the hot sun. It came down to survival, for me and them.

I suggested a plan to Castro, and he jumped on it. We began to put it into motion as soon as we got back to the dump. We went immediately to the head man of the village. His function was to settle disputes over ownership of the garbage. He never went into the dump, but kept a close eye on it from a small hilltop. I had noticed all morning the amount of power he had. His word was law. This was the man we had to deal with.

I had learned, when dealing with Vietnamese, that how

they perceive you is based on how you do business. The actual amount of money being discussed is not important, it's the way you arrive at the final amount that is important. The fact that you will barter over a penny item raises your stature in their eyes. Communism may someday be forced on them, but it will never succeed. Across the barbed wire, two wily businessmen worked out the details of the contract. Through hand gestures, my poor Vietnamese, and his poor English, we struggled to reach an agreement.

From noon 'til about two o'clock is nap time in Vietnam. It is just too hot to work. The whole country, except for the Americans in it, comes to a standstill.

The headman and I negotiated right through nap time. The heads of major companies would have been proud of us. We worked out every detail to the point that neither one of us would lose face.

As everyone returned to the dump after their naps, the head man called them all together. He explained the new rules, and, on the whole, they were accepted by everyone. The few dissenters didn't say anything, but the looks on their faces told me a lot. Like I've said, I'm not much of a talker; I'm more of a listener and observer. People's faces, especially their eyes, can tell you a lot. The eyes I noticed on a few said, "I'm the enemy." Their body postures said, "I will not go along with this, and I will destroy any cooperation between Americans and Vietnamese."

I turned and quietly said to Castro, "Always keep an eye on those two in the back of the crowd." They were old enough to be in the Vietnamese army and weren't. There were several others in the crowd also worthy of keeping an eye on.

The headman finished and approached us. He handed

us five hundred piasters that he had collected from the crowd. The new game in town was about to begin. The rules were these: For five dollars, they could send four of their best runners into the dump to scavenge anything they could carry. When their bags were full, they had to dump it out in front of us , so we could inspect it. Anything of military value to Charlie was thrown back. The crowd had to stay outside the barbed wire, and they had to provide a series of scouts to warn us when the duty officer approached. While the duty officer was present, which wasn't long because of the smell, everyone had to stay out of the dump. At 4:30 the dump was set on fire by the engineers. When we left, the dump was open to all of the villagers. There were a few other rules I will explain shortly.

Let the games begin. Four young men, about fourteen years old took off for the dump. They had quartered the dump for efficiency. Each covered their quarter completely and watched the trucks being unloaded. I'm sure they were pleased with the amount of time they had. One by one, they returned with their bulging bags. When they emptied them out, I almost gagged. There were some things that were still canned, but on the whole, it was garbage. One rule I didn't mention, was that after inspection, the headman would divide the loot on the outside of the barbed wire. Another was, if the duty officer arrives, all bags are left in the dump, and they di di mau out of the dump. We finished out the day at peace with the world. Life was good; smelly and hot, but good.

We prepared for work much differently the next day. We brought a poncho to put over the jeep to protect us from the monsoon rains and the scorching sun. I also brought letter writing materials, and hoped to have time to catch up.

The morning went as planned. I was semi-dry and relaxed. I waved to the headman as I left for lunch. He smiled and bowed, all was right with the world. What happened while I was gone was not my concern.

Late in the afternoon, we had a chance to try out our sentry system. There was only one entrance to the dump, and we had it covered. The duty officer was spotted approaching more than a half mile away. The runners warned the headman, who in turn, warned me. I whistled loudly, and watched four young men scamper through the wire. As senior patrolman, I approached Lieutenant Crego and saluted him smartly. I could hardly keep from laughing, because of the look of amazement on his face. "All quiet on the western front, sir," I said. Time to plant some seeds of thought. "Private Castro seems to have whipped the people into shape. This seems easy enough for one person and the Q.C. to manage," I said. I wasn't saying this for just my benefit. Castro could have a safe year and make a little extra money. The smell soon drove the lieutenant off, but he couldn't leave without one more dumbfounded look over his shoulder. That did make me laugh out loud. I bowed to the headman in the traditional Buddhist manner, and he returned it.

Only one incident marred a perfect week, or as perfect as it could be in a dump. G.I.'s are very superstitious, especially when it comes to death. It was tradition in Vietnam, that when a soldier died, all of his equipment was burned. His personal affects were sent home, but things like his rack, clothing, and boots were destroyed.

This was the only hitch we had in our dump business. The Vietnamese couldn't stand to see this waste. We tried to throw gas on everything and set it on fire, but they outnumbered us. The man I came to call "enemy eyes", snatched some fatigues out of the fire. I was instantly pissed. That S.O.B. was not going to get away from me. I would have had him, but he made it to the barbed wire. He went through and I hurdled over-almost. I snagged my trailing leg. My old football coach wasn't there to yell at me to keep it up. I ripped my pants leg and tumbled to the ground. My Irish temper had me up and moving quickly. If I didn't have my M-16, I would have had him. I followed him on a trail into the jungle. We were now in his world; I should have shot him. I found myself slowing down. Common sense told me to stop. When I did stop, I realized instantly the gravity of my actions. I squatted down to catch my breath, and to make a smaller target. Besides my breathing, I heard nothing, a bad sign. The jungle is usually a very noisy place. As I was planning my retreat, I was watching everything. Not five feet in front of me, at the base of a tree, was something that made my heart skip a beat, and then start to pound in my neck. Facing me was a Claymore mine. The mine sits on little legs with its curved front facing out. In fact, printed in yellow are the words FACE FRONT TOWARD ENEMY, which would be *me*. Many thoughts flashed through my mind, all of them colliding with each other. The uppermost thought was *move*. I jumped over the mine, and behind the tree it was leaning against. Go ahead, Charlie, squeeze the trigger. I knew the tree would absorb the back blast, so I felt relatively secure. When there was no explosion, I carefully peeked around the tree and found out why. The wires to the trigger were gone, and more importantly, the C-4 explosive had been removed from the back. I'm sure some G.I's had removed the C-4, cut it into one inch blocks to cook their c-rations over, and then discarded the mine. What it was doing out there I couldn't, or didn't want to imagine. This all happened before I went into business at the dump.

When I saw I was out of this danger, I ran back down the path to the dump. I knew it was a mistake to retrace my steps, but it would have been a bigger mistake to spend any more time out there. I was more than happy to see this day end.

On my last day of dump duty, one of the village scavengers found a ripped parachute. This created a dilemma. "What would you use it for?" I asked the headman. I had a hard time following his explanation, but as near as I could get, they wanted it for mosquito netting. He pointed at a girl laying on the ground and silhouetted her with his hands. Castro and I didn't fully understand, but what could it hurt? It was panels of pure white silk. "Go ahead, take it," I said. "What do we care, we'll never see it again," I said to Castro. Boy, was I mistaken.

My next assignment was Tropic Lightning Road Patrol. Bill and I were, again, paired together. Tropic Lightning Road is the safest duty there is, even though it was off the base camp. Tropic Lightning Road runs through the village of Ba Ca. Village really isn't the right term. That implies that people live there, and that's really not true when talking about Ba Ca. The village of Ba Ca is a place of business for approximately three hundred prostitutes. The town opens at 8:30 a.m. and closes at 4:30 p.m. Part of our job was to go from store to store making sure everyone, both G.I.s and prostitutes, were gone by 4:30 p.m.. The store fronts were open to the street, and stood side by side on the west side of the street. The husbands and boyfriends of the working girls waited for them on the east side.

At first I viewed this situation as sad, but soon accepted it as another form of survival---their survival and mine. If you treat people with respect, they in turn will often, not always, but often treat you with respect. The girls frequently passed on valuable information about what might happen that night. They may have passed on information to the V.C. also, but like I said, it was a matter of survival.

The V.C. did not interfere with the business being carried on in Ba Ca, other than to collect a tax. They were very careful not to lose this source of income. It was so safe, that no one could carry a weapon in town except the four M.P.'s on duty. The town was located one mile outside the gate of the base camp, but you were probably safer there than when on the base camp. The Americans were in more danger from each other than they were from the enemy. That is where we came into the picture. Wherever there are girls and large amounts of beer, there will be trouble. Mornings were enjoyable, because it took awhile to get drunk. Afternoons could be, and usually were, very long. The Vietnamese girls were not the problem, they didn't get drunk. I was frequently called upon to settle arguments that were shocking and disgusting, usually over sex.

Mama Sans were in charge of their girls, and they ruled with an iron fist. If an argument broke out, it was usually between the Mama San and an American over money and services provided. The arguments were usually very loud, and quickly attracted a crowd of gawkers. It wasn't hard to spot where the trouble was.

I know I will never, ever have that kind of power again. I had total authority to do whatever I wanted. I was the police, judge, and jury rolled into one. When I passed judgment, it was the law. I always tried to be fair, but when dealing with drunk soldiers and Vietnamese women I could barely understand, I sometimes had to make snap decisions. I did this for the safety of everyone involved. I did not want any situation to escalate to the point where someone might get hurt.

If two G.I.'s were fighting, I'd let them get a few blows in. By that time, they were usually ready to quit. If weapons, such as knives or broken beer bottles, were used, I'd get help and break it up a lot quicker.

The mere threat to close a shop down was enough to keep the Mama Sans in line. There was no profit in a closed shop.

That is Ba Ca; the wild west in the far east.

On one particular morning, the first three girls I passed had a vaguely familiar look to them. They wore the traditional Vietnamese dress, called an ao dai. It has a white top with two panels going down to their ankles and is split up the side to their waists. Underneath, they wear black silk pants. The black silk pants weren't what caught my attention, it was the white silk top. I just about choked when I realized their tops were made out of parachute silk. Mosquito netting! Brother, I have got to learn this language better. By the end of the day I had counted over twenty-five girls with the latest in silk fashions.

I knew learning the language was important for my survival, but it would also be helpful to know it to make my job easier. The biggest reason on Tropic Lightning Road Patrol, would be to fight off the unwanted affections from the working girls. As if the thought of thousands of G.I.'s being with these girls daily wasn't enough, I knew I was going to get married to the most wonderful girl in the world when I got home. I was not about to jeopardize that, physically or mentally.

I needed a shield that would not offend anyone. I was discussing this with our interpreter, and he was very helpful. Just say, 'An you em me cong co tien'. After practice, I was ready. Within moments of hitting the street, I saw my first opportunity approaching. In her business there was no time for subtleties. Time is money. "Hey, M.P., you want boom-boom, 3 dolla" she said. I replied in my best Vietnamese, "An you em me cong co tien." She laughed out loud, and before moving on to another customer, she yelled to several other girls. The only part I understood was my shield. They, in turn, passed the message from store to store faster than any telephone service could have sent it. Every store front I passed, I was met with giggles and pats on the arm. An hour later we reached the far side of town, and the message had been there for quite awhile. One of our favorite Mama Sans brought us iced tea for our return trip. We met with two other M.P.'s in a jeep to co-ordinate who was going to eat lunch first. A Mama San touched me and said, "Good boy," and walked away giggling, "An you em me cong co tien."

"What was that all about?" they asked. I explained my situation, and that the magic phrase was, "I love you, but I have no money." That one simple phrase left everyone's honor and respect intact. It also left me with the urge to learn more Vietnamese.

I won't say I became fluent, but I could get the gist of most conversations. I just couldn't get the proper inflections in my voice to properly converse. What I could do is make a list of many important words and phrases and memorize them. Like I've said, I'm a good listener and an even better eavesdropper. What was hard was to not let on that you knew what was being said.

Only two other events on Tropic Lightning Road really stood out. The first one happened because of my stupidity. We tried to keep a jeep patrol moving up and down the street to respond to any problems that the foot patrol might have. We switched jobs to relieve boredom, and it was my turn to drive the jeep. We were at the peak of monsoon season, which meant it rained on and off all day and night for a total of two or three inches a day. The ground was saturated with water.

That sets the scene; next came the stupidity part. As I was driving along, I looked over my shoulder and saw a fight developing. Because of tanks passing by, I couldn't whip a U-turn, so I pulled onto the side of the road. My first clue that I was about to make a mistake should have been the pig wallowing in the mud. By the time I slid to a stop, the pig and I were practically eye to eye. The jeep was buried, over the wheels and partly up the body. I stepped out of the jeep and sunk to over my knees. I told the pig to keep an eye on the jeep, and struggled out to the road. I flagged down a passing tank, and asked the tank commander if he could pull me out. He threw me a rope, and I tied it off to the tank. I then waded back to my jeep. I tied it to the hitch, and struggled back to the driver's seat. "Pig, I'm out of here," I said. Because of all the noise the tank made and all the noise the tank convoy made, it was impossible to hear. I raised my hand to let him know I would drop it when I was ready. What an idiot! I was glancing over my shoulder and lowering my hand when I heard this tremendous roar. Things got a little blurry after that. My head and raised hand were pressed against the windshield. That left the steering wheel buried in my chest. Fortunately, the tank crew untied us, because I couldn't. It took me thirty minutes to get my breathing back to normal, and I had a lump in my chest that I knew was going to be permanent. I'm thoroughly convinced it's the horn buried in there. Before leaving, I took one last look at the pig and wondered if pigs could giggle.

The next event was nothing to giggle about. It was about

three in the afternoon and I was on foot patrol. I was at the end of Tropic Lightning Road when I heard gunfire. To say I was shocked, was putting it lightly. I had gotten to the point where I could recognize the distinctive sound each variety of rifle makes. This was definitely a .45 caliber automatic, a tommy gun, which meant Vietnamese. I went through a store to the back and headed in the direction of the gunfire. I locked and loaded my M-16 and felt for the safety. I then entered the back of the store and crawled to the front. When I snuck a look, I saw a Vietnamese soldier standing in the middle of the street trying to reload. Due to all the screaming and yelling, I figured he must have sprayed the store fronts with bullets. I wasn't about to let him reload, so I placed my bead on his chest and flipped the safety off. I could tell he was drunk from the difficult time he was having getting the clip in. Winging him, I knew, was for the movie audience. I qualified expert with the rifle, so I knew if he got the clip in I would have to shoot his heart out. I had already taken a last breath, in preparation of squeezing the trigger. In fact, I had started the gentle squeeze. My concentration was interrupted by movement at the side of the road. What I assumed was his buddy, approached him from behind with his hands raised. He wanted me to know he was not part of this, but would try to stop it. He did manage to get the weapon away, and I breathed a sigh of relief.

As it turned out, no one was hurt too badly. A few stitches here and there from broken glass, but all in all everyone was very lucky. It was amazing how many people lost their lives because of accidents. You expect people to lose their lives in a war, but not from avoidable, and unavoidable accidents.

I only had two more assignments in the rotation before I started over again. The last two were the most boring.

Hoc Mon Bridge Guard Duty was eleven to twelve hours of boredom. Four M.P.'s at a time would have this duty, with thirty ARVN's backing us up. They were on one side of the bridge, and we were on the other. They had a small fort, and we sat out in the open. Hoc Mon Bridge had been blown up, so our job was to protect the military bridge being used until the new bridge was finished. We had to make sure no civilian traffic was on, or near the bridge when the convoy had to use it. Convoys came through in the morning and in the late afternoon. The rest of the time was spent keeping yourself from going crazy with boredom, which usually translated into getting into trouble. All my life I'd been pretty good at that. As a kid, I was usually at the center of anything exciting. I like to think of it as nervous energy. Nervous energy around explosives and automatic weapons can be, at times, very exciting.

Shooting for me was not just a sport. When I was growing up, it was a passion. My expertise with a rifle was only restricted by the cost of ammunition. Along came the army, and that problem was solved. I've said this before, but if my dad could only see his tax dollars at work. He should be thankful I don't fly a jet fighter.

The land leading up to the bridge on both sides was flooded rice paddies. The hill we were on was the highest point around for miles. We had a pretty commanding view of the area. An enemy force would have to move across four hundred yards of water, rice, and muck to get to us. They would be in our field of fire, with no place to hide, for too long to make it a wise move. We were left alone for most of the time, which gave us lots of time to "work off nervous energy."

Because of all the water, ducks were a common sight. On several occasions, I would lay across the hood of our jeep and shoot one with my M-16. I'd pick one that was sitting on the rice paddy a long way out. I didn't do it to be mean, but it was more of a message to any V.C. out there watching us. At times the ARVN's would want to have a shooting contest, which wasn't much of a challenge. They were the worst shots I've ever seen. Possibly they wanted duck parts for supper and wanted me to provide it. The wager was usually for ten cents and went up with the distance involved. I'd shoot, and most of the time feathers would explode. They would get excited, jabber to each other, and send one of their lowest ranking buddies trudging through the mud to get what was left for their dinner.

Another pastime was shooting rats and scorpions. Every piece of tin or cardboard in the country had either rats, scorpions, snakes, or all three under it. We would flip the trash over and start blasting, usually with our pistols. Scorpion and vermin parts would be flying everywhere. One day I had the brilliant idea to get some tracers from the Vietnamese. A tracer shows its path through the air in brilliant red. Our .45 caliber pistol shot the same bullet the Vietnamese Army used in their tommy guns. A trade was made and the fun began. The first few shots over the rice paddy showed us how inaccurate our pistols were past twenty yards. The pistol had enough power to knock down an elephant, if you could hit it. Oh well, our targets would be within five feet and sneaking across the ground. Since it was my brilliant idea, and I had made the trade, I got to shoot first. The first piece of tin that was flipped produced a huge beady-eyed rat. I laughed out loud as I squeezed the trigger. My laugh was cut short as this brilliant red flash struck the ground and ricocheted straight back, coming within inches of my head. I learned a good lesson there, better not to do that again. Of course, that lesson only covered tracer bullets; hand grenades were a different story.

Every day about ten kids would gather around us. We liked having them around. They were our early warning system. If they didn't show up, you knew you were in for trouble. They, or their parents, knew what was going on. We knew they could never tell us of impending danger, but their presence, or lack of, was warning enough.

I really enjoyed having the kids around, especially a little nine or ten year old Cambodian boy named Bê. Like me, he seemed to have a lot of nervous energy. In other words, he was in trouble a lot. He sold squares of pineapple stuck on bamboo sticks to truck drivers in the convoy. The trucks never stopped, but they slowed down to get on the bridge. He would jump on the side of the truck, and sell the pineapple for anything he could get. The first day I met him, he had one stick of pineapple left after the last convoy of the day, so he gave it to me. It was mouth wateringly delicious. The following day, in preparation for the last convoy, I saw him freshen his pineapple by dipping it in the river. I just about gagged. The Saigon river was a flowing cesspool. I've seen every imaginable thing come floating down that river. Everything from human bodies to water buffalo floated down river, and that was just what was on top of the water! I didn't want to even try to imagine what types of diseases floated along in that water and onto my pineapple. From that moment on when Bê offered me pineapple I told him, "I was saving it for later." After all, if it dried out, I knew how to freshen it up.

Bê and I had lots of fun together, but the thing he enjoyed most was when I would take him fishing. I had the perfect lure, and we always caught fish.

Nap time was the best time to go fishing. Civilian traffic

on the bridge stopped. Military traffic wouldn't come through until 3 o'clock, and I was bored. "Bê, let's go fishing" was all I'd have to say. He would yell to anyone that wanted to fish, to line the banks, or line the bridge. I liked fishing from the center of the bridge best. It was deep. My lure was a hand grenade. I'd pull the pin, let it fly, and duck. The explosion wasn't real loud, because of the depth, but the concussion would bring up many fish. Within split seconds of the explosion, everyone would hit the water. The kids would put one fish in their mouth and one in each hand and swim for shore. Once there, they would secure their supper on a tree limb, and return for more. There is nothing like the relaxation you get from fishing. After collecting their catch, they took off for their village. At night, I could just imagine the fish stories being told around the campfire. Full stomachs bring out some pretty good fish tales.

We couldn't fish all day long, plus, we had to preserve *some* of our ammunition for the war, so there were long periods of boredom, filled with hours of letter writing, trying to stay dry, staring, and dreaming of home and real food. One afternoon I was leaning against the jeep, staring off into space. I vaguely noticed Bê pulling gently on the hair on my arms. I was used to it. He was sitting on the back bench of the jeep, waiting for the afternoon convoy. All Vietnamese are curious about the hair on Americans. Even more interesting to them was our heavy beards. Adults wouldn't do this, but children would lean against you and rub their hand lightly against your beard. They were fascinated, probably because very few Vietnamese have facial hair and none have hair on their arms. The Vietnamese say we Americans speak the language of barking dogs, so all our hair may explain more about our lineage.

Whatever the reason, you get used to it. Bê was always

leaning on my shoulder with his finger tips touching my cheek. If anything, it led to a deeper depth of my staring and daydreaming.

I was snapped out of my melancholy mood by a searing pain in my ear. Bê had caught, and attached to my ear lobe, an inch long fire ant. The pain was unbelievable. I grabbed at my ear and tore the ant off, leaving the head and quarter inch long pinchers buried in my ear lobe. Bill had to pry them out with his knife. The look in my eyes must have told Bê I didn't find it nearly as humorous as he did. There was only one tree on our hilltop, and he was scampering up it, with me close behind. The tree was about thirty feet tall, with a fork about twenty feet off the ground. Bê took the thin limb at the fork. I knew I could reach him from the thicker part, so I climbed further. I knew I had him; I could almost see him splashing into the rice paddy. I reached a little higher with my left hand and leaned out with my right to grab him. I wasn't sure why Bê was laughing, until I felt my hand and forearm catch on fire. He had led me into the perfect ambush. The tree was home to the ant colony, and I blundered into it. I was out of the tree in a flash and burying my arm in the stinking, fetid water of the rice paddy.

What ants didn't come off, had to be pried off. My arm was covered with red welts. At least my arm matched my ear. I told him I was going to keep him in the tree until I had to leave and then the V.C. could deal with him. It was hard to get my point across to him because of all the laughter from him and my so called buddies. Some people sure have a sick sense of humor.

The approaching convoy called for my attention, which allowed Bê his chance to escape. He was also smart enough to work on the far side of the convoy, and he headed for home after it passed.

My hot Irish temper came and went, faster than my welts. Bê was back the next day, but I placed him under strict surveillance. No touching!

The afternoon convoy had a treat for us. I noticed a soldier, riding shotgun on an approaching semi truck, climb through the open roof and move to the trailer. He picked up a box and dropped it to me as he passed. The weight almost broke my back, but it was worth it. It was filled with a treasure we hadn't seen in many months--- a bushel of apples. We pigged out for the rest of the afternoon. There were no apples in Vietnam, but once the kids found out you could eat them and how to eat them, they loved them. They didn't even have a word for apples. We just called it fruit and sent them on their way with a bag full to share with their families. Winning hearts, minds, and stomachs was the name of the game.

The best part of the day was leaving the bridge at the end of the work day. Everyone would probably say the same thing about their job, but this was different. When the convoy security patrol radioed us with the time they would rendezvous with us, excitement was evident on everyone's face. There was a feeling of freedom and exhilaration as we gunned our engines, waiting to pull in behind them. We were all cowboys again, ready for the trail. Of course, there were always a few cowboy yelps as we took off. It was almost as if we were heading up a herd of cattle for the drive to the nearest railroad head. I loved it.

The fact that we were moving gave us some relief from the intense heat. It was interesting to see people in the villages we passed through, relaxing and preparing their meals. I wondered how many were having fish and apples for supper tonight. No one acknowledged our existence as we passed by.

It wouldn't have been wise to show any sign of friendship. Your neighbor might be Viet Cong, and it was getting dark.

The second best part of the day was going to the bridge, for a lot of the same reasons. It was the coolest part of the day, and you were semi-rested, clean, and had a semi-full stomach. The trip out held lots of expectation. Expectation for us was a whole lot different than what most people had as they went to work in the morning. One morning we saw the bodies of two Viet Cong that had been killed that night by an ARVN ambush. They usually placed the bodies in the center of town where kids would place cigarettes in their mouths and place their hands in obscene gestures. The bodies would stay there until their relatives picked them up. With temperatures hitting 115° we hoped they were picked up before our return trip.

Other mornings might show us a monkey or parrot salesman. Sometimes there were snakes for sale. Every morning brought something of interest, something to talk about during the many hours of boredom at the bridge, while waiting in anticipation for the return trip.

One day, the return trip to base camp didn't happen until the next morning. The day began as usual; in fact, it was more boring than usual, until the afternoon convoy. A deuce and a half truck lost its transmission as it was coming off the bridge. Another truck pushed it further off the road so the convoy could continue. After it passed, we discussed what to do with it. That, in itself, was a laugh, thinking we might have a say in the decision making process. Sheriff One brought us back to reality. "What's in the truck?" he asked. Bill yelled to the driver, "What are you hauling?" "Ammo," came the reply. Great, a broken down truck loaded with ammunition, and it would be dark in about three hours. Just in case the V.C. were tuned into our radio frequency, our reply to Sheriff One was, "Material for the Fourth of July celebration." There was a slight delay before he responded, "Gotcha. Stand-by, I'll get back to you." Within a few minutes he was back on the radio. "Hoc Mon, this is Sheriff One. Security patrol will ten one four, your ten one five with further orders. Sheriff One out."

The silence from the radio extended to everyone around it. Finally someone said, "We're in for a long night." Convoy security was coming back to join us. At this time of night, that meant he couldn't get a chinook helicopter or a wrecker. I, like everyone else, began to calculate how much ammo we each had. I wished the fishing hadn't been as good as it was today. I'd have to make sure I carried more tackle from now on. Then it hit me. We had a whole truck load of ammo. That was good and bad news all rolled into one.

For as many hours as I'd spent staring out over the surrounding rice paddies, you would think I would know the area like the back of my hand. The problem is that I was staring during daylight hours. This was going to be totally different. Bill and I were discussing where we were going to spend the night, not from the stand point of comfort, but to make sure we'd get to see the sun come up the next morning. As we were talking, we could see the convoy security jeeps coming down the road at a high rate of speed. When they arrived, there was a lot of laughing and bravado, but you could see the glances out over the paddies and feel the tension.

We started looking at our numbers and at a possible perimeter. There were six bridge guards, twelve convoy guards, two truck drivers and a surprise. After dropping the convoy, the patrol was told by Sheriff One what the situation was. They were then ordered to pick up reinforcements and head back. In

Vietnam, every unit is down to bare bones for obvious reasons, there was a war on. Our Captain had to resort to sending us new guys. Six guys, serving their first day with the company, found out just how far away from home they were.

We paired them up with vets to help them through the night. Bill and I got Pete, an Italian from New Jersey. Pete was smart; he listened to everything we said and asked questions when he didn't understand. We would find out later that he was a fun kid to be around, but now he was all business, as we all were.

Before it got dark, we discussed a few rules. Everyone would stay awake: No talking, moving, smoking, or eating. Total silence, no firing unless it was absolutely necessary. We knew they would test us, to find out where we were. We had no officer with us; the commanding officer would be Sheriff One. He would be over us with another gun ship most of the night. He could provide us with flares, rockets and machine gun fire, but he wanted radio transmissions kept to emergencies only. The highest ranking person on the ground was Sergeant Burch, who had only been in-country for a week. He wanted everyone to know he was in charge, but he was very willing to listen to us. We informed the ARVN fort on the other side of the bridge of our situation, and told them to consider us when they planned their fields of fire.

We discussed whether or not to unload the truck, but decided against it. If they put a rocket into it, it would be a fourth of July celebration like no other we'd seen.

As the sun was setting, we made a great production of moving out into the paddies to set up our perimeter. At an agreed upon time after dark, we would all pull back to our real defensive positions. We hoped this ploy would keep them back for awhile. This tactic meant we had to wade through muck and lay on a paddy dike for what seemed like an eternity. As we lay there staring into the growing darkness, I couldn't keep my mind from wandering. How many centuries had this muck produced rice? What am I doing here? What are we doing here? If I could slap, how many mosquitoes could I kill with one slap? What was crawling up my leg? Question after question as the time passed very slowly.

I looked over my shoulder and could no longer see the outline of the truck. It would be time to move very soon. I hoped the clouds would cover the moon all night. At a prearranged time, Bill tapped me on the shoulder and I tapped Pete. It was time to move out. As quietly as possible, we moved back to the truck and took up our real positions. We must have stirred up every mosquito in the province. There were clouds of mosquitoes preparing to feast all night. For them, it wasn't the Fourth of July, it was Thanksgiving. It was so dark I couldn't see my hand in front of my face. I assumed everyone had made it back to our perimeter. We had failed to set up a password, so I pitied anyone that might be sloshing around out there, lost. If someone was out there, they'd better hunker down low for the night. I was concentrating on the sound of two choppers, high and off in the distance when something splashed in front of us. It was hard to judge how far, but I guessed it was less than a hundred yards out. Charlie was making his first move. He was throwing rocks in hopes we would react with gun fire. The adrenaline was starting to flow by the gallon. Every five or ten minutes a new splash in a different spot.

The monsoon rains had brought the river up and fast. We didn't think they would chance coming by river; it would be too noisy and dangerous, but we had it covered just in case.

They had to know we'd pulled our perimeter in, but they couldn't know how far we'd come in. They also knew there were twenty-six of us, and that we were heavily armed for such a small number. We had six M-60 machine guns, a grenade launcher, and several M-16's. I was on an M-60, and had about 1400 rounds of ammo. The others had the same amount. The question was, how many V.C. had they moved in, in a short amount of time? The cat and mouse game of Vietnam was on.

We knew by the splashing that we were surrounded, but was it by four or five, or a hundred? I didn't really think it was a hundred or they would have tried to penetrate our lines. I thought that they would play with us, waiting for the opportunity to put an R.P.G. into the truck. The ammo cooking off, after the explosive, would probably take care of any of us left after the explosion. Reality is a sickening thing. Darkness worked in our favor. I couldn't see the truck so I'm sure they couldn't.

The clicking noise of bamboo sticks being struck together began, I'm guessing, about 2 a.m. I couldn't see my watch, but it seemed like it was at least two. During one of the torrential downpours, the V.C. had moved closer and were now signaling each other with the bamboo. I'm assuming they were giving their positions and intentions. Each hollow sounding clack went right to the core of my stomach. There were five positions from where the noises came. They were fifty yards or less away. That means they were two paddy dikes out. Did their signals mean they were going to move one closer?

Our noise discipline was excellent, but it was time to make contact with the choppers. Our radio man had covered the entire jeep with ponchos to keep the noise down. He waited for the rain to start again before he made contact. "Sheriff One, this is Hoc Mon. Twenty-five to fifty yards out, we need light. Out" was all that needed to be said. The rain allowed us to send our message, and the V.C. a chance to move forward. We, and they, could hear the approaching choppers, and we all knew what it meant.

I sighted in on the last place I heard them signal and shut one eye to preserve my night vision. The choppers dropped parachute flares which don't last very long, but are heaven to see. The night erupted into gunfire, with red tracers going out into the paddies. I focused on the paddy dike and a few lumps in the rice paddy. The eerie light cast by the flare soon went out, but the twilight zone effect was left in the eye I had open. The firing stopped with the flare going out, and I opened my night vision eye to the claustrophobic darkness. We took a chance lighting up the truck when the flare was dropped, but we hoped the volume of fire would keep their heads down. It worked, there was no return fire.

The rest of the night was relatively quiet. I did throw a hand grenade at what I thought was a reachable noise. The grenade can't be traced back to your position like the tracers from your gun can.

As the gray of dawn finally arrived, we hosed down the surrounding area just to make sure no one was close. When we stopped, we could hear approaching tanks, followed by a wrecker. Road service, Vietnam style.

While they were hooking up the truck, we searched for any sign of Charlie. One blood trail turned up but led into the jungle, and we weren't about to follow it. It could have been laid just to lure us into an ambush, or it could have been Charlie's blood.

That is part of the frustration with this war, the unknown. We had to take satisfaction in the fact that we had survived another night in Vietnam, and we were all one day shorter. As it turned out, it was also the last time I would guard Hoc Mon Bridge. I would cross it one more time, though.

Post Patrol is the last and easiest assignment in the rotation. Officially, we were supposed to respond to any emergency. If we were mortared, we would rush to the area that was hit to restore order and evacuate the wounded. We also would relieve guards so they could eat or change guard duty. Mostly, we went from mess hall to mess hall looking for something to eat, or after dark, we scrounged around for items the company needed. It really wasn't stealing; we were the law, and we would determine if it was stealing or not.

We worked twelve hour shifts during daylight hours for a couple of days, with a day "off" before working a few twelve hour nights. This went on for a couple of weeks.

Not much of those two weeks really stands out except our days "off". We did have several mortar attacks, but very little damage was done. Other than the routine bumps, bruises, and cuts associated with getting into a bunker with twelve other guys at the same time, no one was seriously hurt.

Those twelve guys were your best friends, and would never push you out of the way. But they *would* push you forward if they thought you were moving too slowly! If you're on the outside during an attack, the person in front of you is definitely going too slowly. It's only natural to help him through that two foot by three foot door, and, if he needs help getting down the steps, you're more than willing to help out there also.

Unless you have experienced it, you can't imagine the pure joy and happiness of making it into a bunker.

The adventure begins, usually in the middle of the night, from a sleep that is somewhere between dozing and awake. Your unconscious mind is separating the sound of out-going artillery from the distinctive sound of incoming rounds. Artillery shells passing over your hootch can literally move you and your rack around. Without a conscious thought, the smallest mortar round a half mile away has you and eleven guys up and moving in split seconds. Screen doors are routinely removed from their hinges, and pity anything or anyone that stands in the way. I had trained myself to always lay on my right side, for a faster exit. That was the direction of the bunker. One night, I slipped up. Our poncho liners served as our blankets and they were made of slippery nylon. Needless to say, it caused me to slip and fall. In the dark and panic, eleven guys trampled me into the floor.

Once inside the safety of the bunker, and after taking a head count, the laughter and kidding began. What complete and utter joy! I was alive, no matter what happened next, I was alive now. Live and enjoy life to the fullest.

After two nights of Night Post Patrol, Bill and I would get a day off to perform 'crappy jobs' around the company area. After our day off, we would begin Day Post Patrol for two days, and then begin the process all over again.

I say 'crappy jobs' because one of the jobs was latrine duty. G.I.'s have another name for it. The first time Bill explained what had to be done, I looked at him carefully, hoping he would start laughing and say he was only joking. He didn't, and he wasn't.

Every company area on the base camp had their own outhouse for which they were responsible. Ours was a raised fifteen holer. You talk about losing the urge. Try walking into the outhouse to use it and watch fifteen heads turn your way.

I tried to always go out in the boonies, but that wasn't something you had control over. That was especially true on big, pink malaria pill day. The little white malaria pills, taken every day, have no side effects, but the pink one caused instant cramps and diarrhea. With this in mind, multiply it by 120 soldiers using our fifteen holer everyday. This is where Bill and I came in; twice on our day off. Since there wasn't enough room in Vietnam, let alone on our base camp, to move the outhouses around, all human waste went into fifty-five gallon drums. Our job was to rise early, pull out the full drums, replace them with empty drums and set the full drums on fire. Fuel oil is poured into the barrel and a match is thrown in. After thirty minutes, the contents are stirred and set on fire again. If you have a weak stomach, too bad. Everyone had to do it, at least twice in a year; some had to do it more often.

The good part of this duty, is, that if you got out of the company area without anyone seeing you, you really did get some time off.

There was another hitch to this day. At three o'clock, we had to get a deuce and a half truck from the motor pool, and take the garbage from the mess hall to the dump. After that, we had to return to the outhouse to pull out the full barrels, replace the ones we burned in the morning, and burn the full ones. That concluded the day, except for a thorough scrubbing in the shower.

The first part of the day went as it should have. We left the company area with fifteen huge columns of black smoke spiraling into the sky. Bill and I didn't really have a destination in mind when we set out, but there are very few places on a base camp to go. We hit the PX, where I bought a Time Magazine and some deviled ham and crackers, and we sat in the sun just relaxing and stuffing ourselves. After a few hours, we decided to get a haircut at the post barber shop. For the first time in four months, I felt relaxed. I felt like Beetle Bailey trying to avoid Sergeant Snorkel, so I could loaf.

We arrived at the barber shop at the same time Simari and Norman did. They were the other half of Post Patrol. They had to collect cans of water for the company area. Since there is no running water, water is collected at the water point twice a day, every day. Their job was a lot easier than ours, but we would have it next time.

We laughed about the way we had escaped the company area, but we didn't want to stand out in the open where we could be spotted. We ducked into the barber shop and immediately all the Vietnamese inside yelled "Long mou kek." Simari waved in recognition and moved to an empty chair. Obviously, he had spent some time here, which was understandable. Besides the barbers and shoe polishers there were quite a few pretty girls that did the shaving. "Long mou kek" was not a phrase I was familiar with, so I asked Simari what it meant. "It means pretty boy," he said. One look at this crazy Italian from New York told me he was lying, or he was paying them a lot more than fifty cents for his haircut, shave, polish and massage. I'd make a point of finding out what it meant later.

Three o'clock rolled around and it was time for the garbage run. I had never backed up a truck this large before and was a little nervous. I watched both mirrors and followed Bill's instructions from the loading dock. I backed slowly, as to take in account the height of the truck. I heard the crunching of metal and saw Bill looking up, in my mirror. He hadn't taken into account the height of the truck and the roof of the mess hall.

I hopped out of the truck and saw that the metal roof of the mess hall had been rearranged. The mess hall sergeant was furious. We loaded the barrels of garbage on as fast as we could. As I was pulling away, I had to ask the kitchen help that were standing around watching what "long mou kek" meant. The head Mama San in charge said, through laughter, "That mean nose like eagle."

Pretty boy! Wait until I see that big nosed Italian again. After scrubbing down that evening, we took our lawn chairs out into the middle of the street, where movies were shown every night. Bill, Scotty, Long mou kek, and I sat through one of the last monsoon rains of the year. By the end of the movie, the street was flooded with three to four inches of rain. I never thought I would miss the rain, but once again this country would prove me wrong.

The rest of the week would have been pretty ordinary, except for one incident that would greatly affect the rest of my year.

It was about seven thirty in the evening, and we had just stopped at a luau at the 27th Wolfhounds Company area. They had liberated a small pig from the V.C. and fattened it up on Wheaties and beer. A Hawaiian in their company said he knew how to do luaus, so the party was on. We had just started to dig into our plate full of almost done pork, when the Duty Officer tried to raise us on the radio.

He was furious. A jeep had just passed him going sixty miles per hour, and he wanted the driver arrested because he wouldn't stop. "Yes, sir. We'll get him," I replied. We'll get him when we finish eating, is what I was thinking. Still wiping grease from our faces, we started looking for this criminal that wouldn't stop for the lieutenant.

It didn't take long to find him. Besides our two post patrol jeeps, his was the only other jeep moving on the base camp. We watched him go around the base camp twice while trying to decide what to do about him. We decided to split up. Each patrol would follow him around half the base camp at a safe speed. After all, where could he go? The base camp was a circle, and he'd be bound to run out of gas eventually. We also decided to keep our conversation on the radio to a minimum.

We followed him until dark, around and around the perimeter, until he did run out of gas. As we went up to his jeep, his head was slumped over the wheel, and he was crying.

Sitting behind the wheel was the most frustrated person I had ever met. His best buddy had been killed that day, and he did not know how to deal with his sorrow, anger, and frustration. After a quick huddle, we decided we would put gas in his jeep from our five gallon spare fuel tank. I drove his jeep, and he rode with my partner back to his company area. I talked to his company commander and explained the situation to him. I asked if we could get the Chaplain for him, but the Lieutenant said he would take care of it.

That took care of one lieutenant, but the next one would be more difficult to deal with.

Our agreed upon story would be this: We'd split the two patrols up on the base camp and, as I pulled up to him, I ran out of gas. Anyone could check our spare can and see we were missing a few gallons. While we were trying to get the jeep started, he disappeared.

The story seemed great, until I tried it out on our officer. I could see in his eyes that I had crossed the wrong person. Oh well, what could he do, send me to Vietnam? I was soon to find out he couldn't do that, but he *could* send me further into Vietnam.

August, 1967

The day Post Patrol ended, I was called to the Captain's office. I'd be lying to say I wasn't nervous. I made myself as presentable as possible and reported to him.

"I have a situation I have to deal with immediately," he began. He left me standing at attention as he continued. "Lieutenant Colson feels you disobeyed his orders." Prove it, I thought. "My dilemma is this: your record and the recommendations from all of your sergeants are superior, but I have to work with, and respect my junior officers," he said.

"What I have decided to do is send you to leadership school. After attending leadership school, you will report to the fourth platoon in Dau Tieng," he concluded. "Good luck, and dismissed."

During this whole time I had said nothing and was not asked to say anything. As I reached for the door he said, "Off the record, no problems will follow you up there. You go with a clean slate; in fact, I've sent them a recommendation for your records. Think of this as a way to separate yourself from possible future problems."

"Thank you, sir,... I think," which is exactly how I felt. Many thoughts were racing around my mind as I started packing. There is always fear of the unknown. I had to keep in mind that I was short, and I would soon head back to the world. I would overcome all obstacles. I would survive. Maybe separating me from future problems was a good idea. My buddies helped me pack up and move to the Tropic Lightning Ambush and Leadership School, on the west side of the base camp. We said our good lucks and good-byes, and they left me standing there alone. I sure hoped I would get a letter from Laurie tonight. I needed it.

What I found when I entered the school was twenty-five guys in the same situation. The only difference being, half of them were going back to their old units when they finished the course.

What I didn't know at the time, was that every day from then until the end of my tour of duty would be an adventure. Maybe adventure isn't the right word. I was about to experience the absolute highest highs and lowest lows of my life. I would learn and mature more in the next six and a half months than in the previous twenty-years. The next six and a half months would set my life's path.

The adventure began at the Ambush and Leadership School. I was in school for the better part of August. As I've said, I'd never been much of a student because I couldn't, or wouldn't, recognize the value. But this was a school I could instantly recognize as valuable to me and my survival.

Classes on leadership skills and tactics were held every morning . The classes were held in the morning, when it was as cool as it would get. In the afternoon, everything was hands-on. The first week was on the use and mechanics of various weapons, both American and Communist. We fired every weapon the U.S. Army had in its arsenal, short of nuclear missiles. I had the first hand experience of firing captured V.C.

weapons, from crossbows to 122 millimeter rockets. Our firing range was a no mans land on the north side of camp. From all of the weapons we had access to, I enjoyed, and recognized the value of, the communist AK-47 automatic rifle the most. The American M-16, at this time, was no match for the AK-47. The M-16 jammed constantly. Every G.I. carried a cleaning rod at all times to push out the jammed shells. This was not what you wanted to be doing during a fire fight. There were constant rumors that we would be getting new bolts, which would slow the weapon down and keep it from jamming.

Our final weapons exam was the stripping and putting back together of several weapons while blindfolded. Everyone was given a different weapon for the test. You weren't allowed to know what the weapon would be, so you had to know them all. We had a set, required amount of time to strip it down and put it back together again. My weapons exam was an AK-47 and a .50 caliber machine gun. The AK was a piece of cake, but the size of the machine gun slowed me down. I managed to make it in time, but just in time. That phase of my training was over.

The first sergeant congratulated us on the first phase and explained the second phase:

Mornings were spent learning ambush and booby trap tactics, theirs and ours.

Afternoons were spent in explosives training. (Be still my beating heart, did he say explosives?)

That last week, we put everything we'd learned into practice. The idea of the school was to experience everything you might have to ask someone else to do. Experience is always the best teacher. Someone can explain and you'll learn, but it's never the same as first hand experience.

That's enough said. Let's blow something up.

Ambush tactics and especially booby traps were very interesting, but everyone wanted to get to the loud stuff.

We had all taken our seats in a thatched lean-to with no walls, in hopes of catching a breeze. The instructor got our attention immediately by setting off a small detonation using remote control. He really didn't have to do that; we were all primed (excuse the pun) and ready to go.

That afternoon, we worked our way from hand grenades to mines, simple stuff. The following day got more complicated, and more interesting. As half of our group provided security, the other half cleared trees further and further from the perimeter wire with explosives. We wrapped C-4 plastic explosives, detonation cord, and dynamite around several large trees. After yelling, "Fire in the hole," they went down, up, and in every direction in a flash. After they were down, bulldozers pushed them into a pile. We then placed Bangalore Torpedoes into the pile and set them to explode. The six foot, tubed explosive was quite often used to cave-in tunnels or blow up strands of barbed wire. The pile of trees was spread out because of the explosion, repiled, and blown up again. Each time we experimented with shorter and shorter fuses. It reached the point where it was getting dangerous. By the end of the day, I was covered with slivers and splinters. Timing was everything.

We also placed several types of mines and were told the next day that we had to find them, disarm them, and bring them back. We were always broken into groups of three's for every exercise. Each group had to exchange maps of their mine field with another group and had to find their mines. This added a little stress to the job. When you draw your own map, it's clear to you, but is it clear to everyone? We used the map to get close and then used our training and common sense to finish the job. There were no accidents. We were all good students who wanted to learn.

The last week of the school we flew to a captured village and looked for booby traps. We had trained in a village on our base camp and had "lost" three during the search of that village to nonlethal booby traps. It was a thorough training of every type of booby trap we might run into, or hopefully not run into.

One of the most ingenious traps was a jeep spring, fashioned into a crossbow. The "arrow" was a six foot, one inch steel rod. The trigger was set off by the backwash of a helicopter. Because of the few landing zones available, the V.C. knew that a helicopter would eventually make a landing in the opening they had chosen. They were right; the helicopter that set off the booby trap had a steel rod pass right through its tail. No one was killed but there was considerable damage done to the chopper.

Our search of the captured V.C. village was under the very watchful eyes of our instructors. They had been through the village already to make sure they didn't lose any students. Field trips were always exciting.

We found and marked most of the booby traps in short order. We also found a bonus. As another guy and I entered a hootch, I noticed a fire going, which struck me as odd. It was too hot to be needed for heat and too early to prepare food. I took my bayonet and poked into the ashes. A metallic clink sounded under the ashes. Very carefully, we put the fire out and removed the ashes. This exposed a metal plate. Before lifting it, we called Sarge over. We needed an expert. With someone on all four corners we lifted a three foot by three foot steel slab up and out of the hootch. Underneath the plate, a tunnel was exposed. "What now?" I asked. Sarge said, "We'll call in tunnel rats to check it out. You haven't covered tunnels yet. That will be next week."

I looked down at that tiny hole disappearing into darkness, and then looked around the hootch at the others and felt my stomach tighten.

As a kid, we had made underground forts with tunnels leading to them, but I never liked them. Our tunnels went about five feet to a fort that was no more than a covered hole in the ground.

What I was looking at was a hole that went further down than I wanted to think about. We had been told that the final week of school would be the time we put everything we had been taught into practice. We began the week with tunnels. It was explained to us that the 25th Infantry Division Base Camp had a tunnel under it that it used for training. That's one tunnel we knew about, out of many we didn't know about.

Tunnel rats were responsible for searching tunnels, and we found miles of tunnels during our operations. Tunnel rats were always wiry little guys that had volunteered for this dangerous duty. After finding a tunnel, a rat, along with his trusty pistol and a flashlight, disappeared underground. The tunnels had many levels, and were full of booby traps, dead bodies, filth, the enemy, and most of all, darkness.

The reasoning behind sending us underground was: Don't ask someone to do something you wouldn't do.

We were handed a pistol and a flashlight, and were told we would start going through the tunnel in ten minute intervals. I wanted to get it over with right away, so I volunteered to go first. As it turned out, I went second.

While waiting my turn, I was told, always go forward. Do not use your flashlight unless you need it; we want you to experience a real combat situation. The pistol is unloaded, but always carry it in a firing position. When you do turn your light on, hold it to the side so the enemy will fire at the light. That all seemed logical when you were standing in the sun, but when you were standing twenty feet straight down looking up at the tunnel opening, logic was the last thing on your mind.

Where the tunnel turned horizontally, I tried to position my big American body so I could get in. The hole was less than two feet high and wide. A Vietnamese could crawl on hands and knees, but I was reduced to a belly crawl. I was all of fifty feet into the tunnel when I could feel my first brush with panic. My breath was coming faster and harder. I knew the tunnel was almost a mile long, and I'd already lost track of how far I'd come. I'd never had claustrophobia, but was beginning to experience it. I just had to have more room. Just as I thought I'd lost it, I burst into a room. The room was approximately ten feet wide and twenty feet long, with an exit tunnel at the far end. I shined the flashlight around and found I could almost stand up. I crossed the room and shined my light down the tunnel. I turned the flashlight off to preserve the batteries, and crawled as far and as fast as I could. I had to stop and catch my breath, but felt I'd made it quite far along the tunnel. When I flipped the light on, it almost made it worse, as I could see how close the walls were. All those, "What if?" questions started popping up in my mind. The biggest one was,"What if the tunnel caved in?" Stop, don't think like that! I looked at myself and saw I was coated with red clay. I gave thought to taking my shirt off so I would slide better, but then I remembered the instructor saying that the beginning of a panic attack was when you start to shed clothing. He was right. I truly believe I was on the verge of a panic attack. I had to get out.

I went forward in a spurt, and felt I was saved from insanity by another large room. I didn't dive into the exit tunnel quite as fast this time. I tried, once again, to gain control of my thoughts, but then I felt the room closing in on me. Once more, I dove into the exit hole, and was determined to push to the end. I was getting out of this hell. I was fast approaching the point of sheer terror. All that good advice I'd been given up where the sun shone, now didn't mean a thing. I put the flashlight in my mouth and my pistol in my waistband in the small of my back. "If they want to shoot at the flashlight, at least this way they'll hit me between the eyes, and this will be over," I thought.

I had crawled so far and so fast I thought my heart would explode. I had to rest, so I shut the light out and closed my eyes to shut out the dark. For the rest of my life, if I ever run into a tunnel rat, I will bow to him in respect. It seemed like a crazy thought, but it helped. I will also kill anyone that tries to put me underground ever again. It had better be a grave, or we're all going under together.

How do the V.C. do it? They've been digging tunnels since before the French were here in the 1950's. I wouldn't doubt that they were digging under Japanese base camps during World War II.

The musty damp air wasn't reviving me too fast, so I had to move on. When I opened my eyes in the dark, I could see a pin prick of light somewhere way off in the distance. I could have cried; I may have. After that final push and short scramble up, I was bathed by the warm sun. I felt like I was reborn. After sitting there, regaining my composure, I thought to myself, "You've pushed your body and mind to a point it's never been."

This trial of body and soul has given me the confidence to say, "I feel I can accomplish anything I put my mind to," and even more importantly, the confidence to say "I won't do it," if I don't want to. Maybe that was the point of the whole exercise. I would decide which battles were worth fighting from now on.

I still thought I was fighting for a good cause, but I began to wonder why we were trying to push an 18th century country into the 20th century. I was just a high school graduate, with only six months in-country, but I'd started having doubts about this war after only three months. Surely those geniuses in Washington D.C. knew more than I did. I wished I could have them crawl through that tunnel to see the dedication the enemy must have. I hope this wasn't a case of good intentions gone bad.

We got the rest of the day off to relax, which had me a little worried. Why?

We soon found out why. Once again we were divided into three man teams, with one team of fifteen. Every three man team would rotate through the larger team until everyone had accomplished three objectives.

The big team was an ambush team that would set up every night. We would stay on this until our three man team came up for a listening post and a compass course exercise.

Three nights in a row we went out, through the wire, to set up in the jungle. It was to a different spot each time, but the procedure was always the same. Inspection, to make sure no one rattled or might have an item that could possibly shine and give our position away. Silence was essential. Patience, as it turned out, was the most important aspect of our three days. Nothing happened.

Our three man listening post was a new experience.

After dark, we low- crawled out through the wire about fifty yards, to sit all night. It was, as the name implies, a listening post. We were not there to engage the enemy, unless we had no choice. If it ever came to that, we wouldn't stand a chance.

The idea was to put ears further out than the wire, to act as an early warning device. If the enemy was detected moving about, the handle of the radio microphone was squeezed. No one spoke, and no one called. If we squeezed the handle, warning the bunker line, our next move was to get as low as possible, because the bunker line could open up at anytime. Normally, we would have walked out, but the moon was really bright. As passing clouds covered it, we crawled further and further out. Every time the moon cleared, we froze until we could finally move. We came to a slight depression, and all three of us got into it, back to back for the night. It didn't take long for the mosquitoes to find us and make us totally miserable. Well, not totally miserable, that was still to come.

I will never understand to where all the monsoon rain water disappeared. All that mud had turned to red dust. Since I was nervous and sweating, the dust stuck. I must have looked like the pink panther. To make matters worse, the wind started to pick up. It seemed like a gale force wind. We pulled our jungle hats down over our faces, and put as much of our M-16's under our shirts as we could. It didn't blow long, but a lot of the province was moved into our little depression, and onto us. We stayed perfectly still so we wouldn't lose our camouflage. My only fear was that a Viet Cong would crawl up behind this new mound and use us for cover.

When dawn finally broke, and we emerged from the mound, we had to laugh at our appearance. Oh well, I was one day shorter.

The final assignment was held a day later. Once again, most of this exercise took place at night. It was never said, but I believe part of the school's intention was to make us feel comfortable with the night. If it wasn't the intent, it was an added bonus. I now know how to use the night, and I will always look at it differently than when I was a civilian. Night can be your worst enemy, but also your best friend. In our course work the previous week, we had covered compass use, long range recon, and escape and evasion. We were about to put it all to use. Our three man team, along with an instructor, would follow a series of compass settings to a designated spot and return by morning. The instructor's position was one of support, if we needed it. He was there to call in air support and answer questions, if we would lower ourselves to ask.

We were given our map and the co-ordinates we were to follow, and the rest was up to us. We quickly put our equipment together, and met back at the lean-to to plan. We knew we had to travel light and fast. Our weapons were two M-16's, with each person carrying two hundred rounds of ammo, and one M-79 grenade launcher. We didn't include the instructor's M-16 in our inventory.

We had decided to eat our c-rations before we left, so we wouldn't have to carry food or worry about potential noise. We would all carry water; that was a necessity.

While we were eating, we applied camouflage paint to to our faces and checked each other for noise and shine.

We were trying to hurry, to make use of the daylight. We wanted to get as far as we could along our "course" before dark. Sitting through the night didn't bother me as much as the thought of trying to follow a compass course in the dark. I had been orienteering in the states, and it was fun, even at night. This was entirely different; success was determined by coming back alive. If we reached our objective, that was an added bonus.

We moved out at about 4:30 p.m. Before getting serious with the compass, we had to lose the eyes that were always watching from the surrounding jungle. We had joined a work detail, clearing the jungle further back from the base camp's perimeter. One by one, we slipped into the jungle and waited for the detail to move away.

As soon as safely possible, we took a reading and moved out. We were making good time, although it would be considered slow from a civilian's prospective. We had covered almost two clicks when we ran into a snag. Our co-ordinates were going to take us right past a small hamlet that was not shown on our map. Should we wait until dark, and stay the course, or should we move out and around this hamlet? Did we screw up or were the horror stories about maps of Vietnam true?

The hamlet consisted of five or six thatched huts and an assortment of farm animals. I don't think thirty people in total lived there.

The sun was setting, so we decided to take a reading, wait until things quieted down for the evening, and then we would move through. We were hidden pretty well, and from our vantage point we could watch the hamlet settle down for the night. It was a peaceful setting. People were moving about, talking with each other; children were playing and meals were being prepared. I couldn't help wondering if it was really as peaceful as it appeared.

We plotted our route along the hamlet, running it over and over in our minds. We were ready. About midnight we started forward. There was a half moon, so we moved from shadow to shadow. I was on point, so it was my responsibility to avoid the flock of geese they used as an alarm system, and more importantly, to avoid the water buffalo. Water buffalo attacked Americans. I had been told it was because we eat meat, and the Vietnamese are predominately vegetarians. Little kids, eight years old, watched the family herd. They rode them and hit them with a switch, and the buffalo ignored them. Let an American come near and watch out. The ears went back and the head started to lower. I didn't need an enraged bull chasing me through the jungle.

We passed through the hamlet without alerting anyone and moved further along our set course. With the use of hand signals, we decided it would be best to wait for first light before going further. We weren't sure how much longer this would take, and we were very tired. We decided to sleep in shifts.

It seemed as though I had just shut my eyes, when I felt the gentle touch to inform me it was my shift. My shift was spent listening to the sounds around me. I tried to identify the creatures of the night, but I was making wild guesses. What I did know was that most of these sounds would not be heard in Michigan. My shift ended, and I was sound asleep in seconds. My sleep ended abruptly with a terrifying scream, not from me, but almost. A very large animal was eating a smaller animal. My hope was that the smaller animal was enough to fill the larger animal. Whatever the case, we would all stay awake until dawn. The entire time, my imagination put tigers in every shadow.

At first light we took a reading and started to move out. We hadn't gone fifty yards, when I felt something swinging on my neck. I reached to my neck and felt a slimy object about the size of a marble swaying back and forth. We were covered with leeches and had to take time to get them off. One by one we stripped down and poured salt over the leeches. Our instructor had been there before and had come prepared. I'll never understand how something as gross and slimy as a leech can get on you, suck your blood, and you never feel it until it has gorged itself on your blood.

Our designated spot was a place where two creeks joined into one, which we found about mid-morning. The return route was of our own choosing, which meant the shortest route possible. We did not want to spend another night in the boonies. Besides a few bananas, we hadn't eaten anything for quite awhile. I'll have to make a mental note: Always take something along for emergencies. The trip back was uneventful. We made the trip fast enough to be careful, and no faster. We walked through Ambush Gate about 6 p.m. I had graduated from the 25th Infantry Division's Tropic Lightning Leadership and Ambush School, and I was proud of myself. It may seem silly, but I'm as proud of that diploma, maybe more so, than I am of any degree I have or will ever have.

September, 1967

September found me in Dau Tieng, Viet Nam. This base camp, located in the Michelin Rubber Plantation, was home to the Third Brigade of the 25th Infantry Division. It was in War Zone C, near Cambodia. The convoy ride in told me all I had to know about Dau Tieng. It was out in the boonies, and it was dangerous.

The base camp itself was a one mile long by half mile wide oval, with an air strip in the middle. The southern half of the base camp was covered with rows of rubber trees and a beautiful plantation house. It wasn't hard to figure out why we were there, and what we were protecting.

On the southwest side of the base camp, the village of Dau Tieng came right up to our perimeter wire. The village housed the rubber workers and was fifty to sixty percent Viet Cong. One mile from our main gate was the Michelin Rubber Factory. The only bridge crossing the Saigon River into the village, was located near the factory entrance. The street from the factory to the main gate was lined with brick homes. These homes belonged to the Michelin Company and housed their office help and foremen. A company of soldiers protected the factory, water tower, and bridge at all times.

The north and east side of camp led into the Michelin

forest, row after row of fifty foot tall rubber trees. I was told the plantation spread into Cambodia.

Base camp strength was said to be 1,500 soldiers, but I doubt it was ever over a thousand. Other than M.P.'s, very few Americans were allowed off base.

Our platoon's two hootches were located between the plantation house and the chopper pad. Rubber trees shaded our entire compound. In fact, my hootch was built around two rubber trees to avoid cutting them down. The trunks went right up through the tin roof. Our mess hall was the headquarters company mess hall, located one hundred yards from my back door.

I knew the choppers on our west side would be a target for V.C. mortars, but there were benefits that balanced the location out. The plantation stable had running water. There weren't any horses, so people lived in the stable, and we could shower where they used to wash horses. The plantation house itself was a beautiful French colonial mansion. A wall surrounded the manicured grounds. A Vietnamese man and his daughter were the caretakers and were allowed to stay overnight. They, and a few interpreters, were the only Vietnamese allowed on the base camp overnight. The house and grounds were always immaculate. A Michelin manager would come and spend only two days out of the year there, but the mansion was always ready for occupation. One big problem was the swimming pool. Because it was within the walls of the plantation, many people didn't know it was there. It was considered a court martial offense if you were caught on the grounds, and we had to enforce the law, which meant we went swimming fairly often during the middle of the night. Before I left Dau Tieng, the mansion would be destroyed.

My hootch had fourteen guys and one monkey in it. My rack was second from the door. Position was based on how short you were. In-country short, not physically. Close to the door meant close to the bunker.

My four foot by six foot living area contained my canvas cot, mosquito netting, wood crate shelf, foot locker, lawn chair, and my prized possession, a fan. Our electricity was tied into the plantation's electricity, so we had power all night. We couldn't have lights on after dark, but tape recorders and fans ran all night.

On my first night, after meeting the guys and having chow, I was called in to meet Lieutenant Jones. Everyone had informed me on what to expect, and they were right. Jones didn't, what you would say, command respect. He was a second lieutenant from Maryland or Virginia, a school teacher. If he ran his class the way he ran this platoon, he wouldn't last in the teaching profession very long. We went through introductions and expectations, and I was soon dismissed.

I then went to see the person that really ran this platoon, Sergeant First Class Williams, but everyone called him Papa-San. Papa-San had twenty-nine years in the U.S. army, and this was his last year. He had been promised another promotion for another year, but he wouldn't do it. Papa-San had been through World War II and the Korean war, but he didn't like the way this war was being fought. This was a man who cared deeply about the men for whom he was in charge. The respect was mutual.

Killed and wounded soldiers affected any Lieutenant's career; they tore at the very soul of Papa-San. Papa-San was the kind of leader for whom you would do anything, and follow anywhere, because you knew he wouldn't ask if it didn't have to be done. Papa-San led by example. If there was a dangerous assignment, he would be right there along side of you.

Lieutenant Jones, on the other hand, only left the base camp when he was forced to. That amounted to once in six months, and that turned into a disaster. I doubt he ever talked to a Vietnamese the entire time he was in-country. I also believe I've never felt such contempt for a fellow human being. I had, and still have, more respect for the Viet Cong than I do for Lieutenant Jones.

As Papa-San gave me the grand tour, I got my first introduction to the local Viet Cong. The first mortar round landed thirty yards away on the chopper pad. The second round exploded in the trees above our hootch. The third round landed behind me, much too close. I was bent over at the waist, entering the bunker, when I found myself lifted into the air and thrown against the back wall. When I came to, the mortar attack was over. I pushed someone off me, and in the fading light of sunset, I could feel and see that I was covered with blood. Fortunately, after a frantic search, I found out it wasn't mine. The concussion from the round threw me and the guy behind me into the bunker. He had some shrapnel wounds, not very serious, just painful. I had a lump on my head and was bruised, but I had survived the evening. The night wasn't over.

About 1:00 a.m. Papa-San woke my squad up and told us to get dressed and meet by the jeeps. When we were all gathered he said, "Earlier today, a G.I. had an argument with his girlfriend, a Vietnamese worker, and, after drinking too much, had decided to go to her house and apologize. He is in the village, and, if he is still alive, we have to bring him out." Our plan of attack would be one based on speed. We would, as fast as possible, drive our jeeps to the house, knock the G.I. out if we had to, and beat it back to camp. Three of us would enter the house, and the rest of us would provide security.

Lieutenant Jones followed us down to the gate, and his last words of encouragement were, "Remember: Do not load your weapons." As the jeeps lurched forward, I thought I had just been electrified. I couldn't believe what I had just heard. "What did he say?" I said. "Was he kidding?" My answer was the sound of M-16's being locked and loaded. I knew I was going to like these guys.

We retrieved the soldier without incident, and he spent the next twenty-four hours in our Conex-box jail. The "jail" was a five foot high, by six foot wide, by six foot long shipping container. A six inch by six inch barred window provided the only light and circulation. Calling it a sweat box is a very accurate description. It may seem cruel, but I only saw it used twice in six months and both times it served its purpose.

Within a week, I had gotten into the routine of Dau Tieng. Our platoon was broken into four squads of ten to fourteen men each, and one monkey. Each squad had an assigned responsibility for one week long periods. For the rest of September, I would move from assignment to assignment at random. If someone was sick, wounded, or on R & R, I took their job. This would give me a quick introduction to the different jobs and a chance to get to know everyone in the platoon. Since two squads were always working nights, it was hard to get to know people in the other shifts.

The two squads on day shift were divided up to cover two checkpoints, Town Patrol and Post Patrol. Post Patrol was divided up even further. They were responsible for covering the post and also for searching the Vietnamese workers when they came in, and when they left for the day. Post Patrol would also direct convoys onto the base camp and lower the flag in the evening.

The two squads on night duty were also divided up. One squad would post guard on the headquarters area, guard any POW's we had, and Post Patrol. The other squad had roving Ambush Patrol. This squad would move around the village all night, trying to stop the V.C. from collecting taxes and kidnapping people, usually kids, to act as pack animals.

Any "spare" time was spent doing the usual: filling sand bags, latrine duty, scrounging materials, and cooking.

Since the mess hall food was nothing more than larger portions of c-rations, we often cooked our own meals. When we were on base camp, we ate breakfast and lunch at the mess hall, but quite often prepared supper ourselves.

Barbecues of water buffalo steak and liberated chicken were common. Frequently meals were planned around mail call.

Food from home was always shared. Our squad had guys from all over the United States, and we were as diverse as you can get. We received coffee cans full of tortillas, home made Italian sausages, Wisconsin cheese, and ham. A neighbor of mine from back home sent a coffee can full of fudge. That night we had tacos and fudge soup. One hundred degree heat changed the shape, but did not effect how quickly it was slurped up.

Our hootch girl would often buy us vegetables at the market, and we would share our meals with her. Ba, which means older lady, was what she wanted to be called. She was our mother far from home. She swept and cleaned up after fourteen slobs, and she deserved more than the one dollar a day she received as pay. Any meals we had, she took part in, and leftovers went home with her. I would have loved to have heard her explanation to her family of what was for dinner every night.

Ba ate with us, and, of course, so did Charlie. Charlie was a one foot tall monkey, cute as a bug, but mean as a scorpion. He had his own high chair at our table and sometimes he sat in it. Most of the time he would walk on the table, picking at the food that looked good to him. If he saw something he liked on your plate, you had better beat him to it, or there was bound to be a fight. Once he had his hands in your plate, you risked being bitten if you tried to reclaim it. Just getting your plate back was tricky. You had to wait for someone else to get up, and then use their plate to lure him away. Since our hootch was full of strange and exotic bugs, you could send him off on a hunting trip.

Spotting a huge Praying Mantis crawling on the ceiling, I would tap him on the shoulder and point up. Charlie would scan the rafters until he found what I was pointing at. Cat like, he would sneak up on the bug, snatch it, and chomp it down like a banana. I'm not so sure that says much about our meals; he preferred raw bugs to our tacos.

Frequently, while still in the rafters, he would whiz on us or worse. If he wasn't aiming at us, he had to be the luckiest shot in all of southeast Asia. With all the weapons around, I'll never understand why he lived as long as he did.

Besides Charlie, we had two dogs, Lifer and Snowflake. Lifer looked like he had some German Shepherd in him, but he was mostly a mutt. Lifer was a true veteran. He could distinguish incoming shells from outgoing shells. Like us, he would sleep right through an hour of outgoing shells, but let one incoming round hit and he was up and running for the bunker. He was frequently the first G.I. in the bunker and was just as excited as we were to be there.

Snowflake, on the other hand, had seen far too many attacks; she was shell shocked. As the name implies, she was pure white, but the guys jokingly said she used to be black. She turned white from fear. If you observed her for awhile, you would be inclined to believe it. At the sound of the first "crack" of enemy mortars, she flopped on the floor, shaking and drooling. You couldn't help but feel sorry for her unless you tripped over her in the dark on your way to the bunker. Any loud noise, even the stomp of a foot, would send her into convulsions. Within minutes, she returned to the sweetheart she was.

One unique feature about our hootch, besides the trees growing in it, the bugs, and the monkey, was our refrigerator.

Its uniqueness was based on the fact that we had the only refrigerator, other than the mess hall's, on the base camp. We decided to get the refrigerator one night after a mortar attack. Our club, which amounted to a twenty foot by twenty foot shack with an ice cooler, closed after dark. Beer and pop were ten cents, when it was open. It closed when it got dark. That left the rest of the night, during which we were often awake and thirsty. A refrigerator was the only solution to our problem. From decision to plug in took about one week.

The first step was making the deal. We had to find a chopper pilot that made round trips to Saigon. That part was easy. Choppers flew supplies, mail, and ammo, up to us. They took wounded soldiers and G.I.'s going on R & R back to Saigon every day. These kinds of deals in the Army required no money on our part. The pilot wanted twelve AK-47's in trade for the refrigerator.

We had the negotiated, captured weapons gathered

before he was ready to fly back to Saigon. On Friday, when he returned, we had a refrigerator. The refrigerator held two cases of beer, and the pilot had a thousand dollars in his pocket. He sold each weapon for a hundred dollars to some Saigon G.I.s who wanted a souvenir. Everybody was happy.

Every night before going to bed, we covered the refrigerator with our flak jackets. After mortar attacks we felt pretty smug as we popped a cold one and toasted each other for the luck we had. Life was good.

After tucking our refrigerator in for the night, we frequently sat outside in the dark shooting the bull. We hoped to catch that nonexistent breeze and just pass some peaceful moments acting like the teenagers we were.

As we sat around drinking our pop and beer, the mosquitoes attacked in unbelievable numbers. We'd all put on mosquito dope, but had sweated that off within minutes of putting it on. We kept putting it back on until Korean Carl made his appearance. Korean Carl was one of many Korean nationals hired by the Army to carry out odd jobs around the camp. They ran the water station, did some tailoring, and ran the P.X. They also sprayed the camp for mosquitoes. Every night during the dry season, they would climb into a truck with a turret that was attached to a large chemical tank. The spray from the turret was like a fire hose. It could shoot mosquito dope one hundred and fifty feet and create a cloud of throat clogging, eye watering, death for mosquitoes.

One day, as Korean Carl was about to spray us, I casually asked, "Do you think that spray can hurt us?" Before I got an answer, we all covered our beer, held our breath and closed our eyes. As the cloud of spray settled on and around us, soaking our skin, I gave more thought to this practice. The spray was strong enough to keep mosquitoes away for three or four hours. We were covered with it nightly, even when we slept.

"What do you think? Is this stuff safe? We can't hold our breath long enough, so we breath it in and it covers our skin," I stated, as the cloud disappeared.

Wicklow said, "It has to be. It's probably like agent orange. We get sprayed with that too, and no one's died, or grown a third eye or anything."

"You're probably right," I said, without fully believing, but happy to have the mosquitoes gone.

During the month of September we had a seven day truce, which allowed us time to repair and prepare for its end. The V.C. used truces to resupply. We always paid for it in the long run.

The only other assignment I had for September was Checkpoint Three. Three roads entered Dau Tieng, and checkpoints were set up on all of them. We, and a group of ARVN's, covered two of the checkpoints. The Bridge Guard Company covered the third road. The ARVN's and their families lived in a huge barb wire enclosed bunker at this checkpoint. Three M.P.'s were assigned to help during daylight hours. Our mission was to search people as they entered and left town. We were looking for medical supplies, large quantities of food, money, fake I.D.'s---in other words, any contraband the enemy could use.

The road into town ran across a one mile open field. The road was raised up about fifteen feet, and no one was allowed off the road. When I say they weren't allowed off the road, I mean shoot first and ask questions later. At least a couple times a day the ARVN's would shout out the only English they knew,

"Inside, inside," and we would scoot through kids, chickens, and garbage to the second floor where we would stare and fire where they pointed. Since we had more ammo than they did, we pumped a lot of lead into the jungle. I never did know how they knew anyone was out there, or more to the point, if anyone was out there.

Besides these occasional one sided fire fights, Checkpoint Three was pretty boring. During the Vietnamese nap time, the Americans just roasted in the sun waiting for whatever. During the rest of the day, we just roasted in the sun, also.

With the end of September, I was under 180 days.

October, 1967

By October we were into the dry season. The next time it rained, I'd be packed and ready to head home. Every morning began the same way. Up at 4:30 or 5:00 a.m., trying to get the nights layer of red dust off. We cleaned up at a wash basin outside of our hootch. The cold water woke you up quickly, but it made shaving a real chore. Then it was off to the mess hall for rice and c-rations. Ham and lima beans at 5:30 in the morning doesn't cut it. Come to think of it, it didn't cut it at any other time of the day either. It was rice and C-rations for every meal. After breakfast, we all moved to our duty stations. For me, during this first week of October, it was Checkpoint Four. Checkpoint Four was much more exciting and dangerous. Our mission was, once again, searching everyone that entered or exited the village. For the most part, they were workers from the Michelin Factory going out to harvest rubber. We were looking for any form of contraband.

The checkpoint was located three-quarters of a mile from the east side of our base camp. One quarter mile further east was an ARVN bunker. We chose this spot between the base camp and the bunker because there was a football field size opening in the rubber trees. We would eventually enlarge this opening to keep the V.C. further back, but it would take a few attacks before we got permission to cut any trees. We had two sand bag bunkers across the street from a Catholic church and school. One bunker was close to the road. The other bunker was forty yards back, close to the rows of rubber trees. The back bunker contained a squad of infantrymen, who covered our backs. The front bunker had three M.P.'s and an interpreter. Two guys covered the other two on the road, and we switched places every hour.

Just getting to the checkpoint was a thrill. As soon as it was light enough to see, four to six machine gun jeeps would race out to the checkpoint. Just before reaching the checkpoint, we would break off into different positions. We tried not to do the same thing everyday, but there was only so much you could change. One jeep would go north on a two rut road that ran along the length of the rubber trees. A second jeep went past the checkpoint. That covered our left and right flank. The other jeeps approached the bunkers, looking for an ambush or booby traps that might have been set up during the night. Both happened frequently.

When it was time to leave at night, we did the same thing in reverse. As soon as the sun set, everyone drove as fast as possible back to the base camp.

Once we secured the area in the morning, and we were all in place, the extra jeeps would head back to camp. Occasionally, throughout the day, they would check back with us, and then stay in constant radio contact with us.

Shortly after we were settled in, the Michelin workers started arriving by truck. Searching people in the morning was much better than after they had been working all day in 110 degree heat. Of course, by the end of the day we didn't smell so great either. On some days we would get a break. The V.C.

would keep the workers all night to "reeducate" them. These poor people just wanted to get a day's work in, and we hassled them one way, and the V.C. hassled them another way.

From 11 a.m. until 3 p.m. was the slowest part of the day. We tried to keep our minds occupied by writing letters, catching frogs and snakes, and playing cards. At this checkpoint you couldn't shoot or blow things up, because it would bring a reaction force from the base camp. This led to long stretches of pure boredom, punctuated by moments of sheer terror.

Before the end of the year, two good events happened at Checkpoint Four.

The first took place while I was on duty at the checkpoint. Every morning I noticed a young woman pushing a bicycle through the front yard of the Catholic church, thus avoiding our checkpoint. Since we were primarily concerned with the workers going out into the rubber plantation, and she was headed into town, we left her alone.

Toward the end of the week, my curiosity got the best of me. I asked our interpreter to come with me so I could question her. When we approached her, I couldn't help noticing she tipped her head so her face was even more concealed by her conical hat. Through the interpreter, I found out she was a teacher in Dau Tieng. She avoided the checkpoint because she was embarrassed by her looks. It was then I noticed a raw patch of skin on her neck. She wouldn't show us her face, but said it was worse than her neck and was spreading. I told her she could see our medic, and he might be able to prescribe some medication for her. They had medicine for everything that could be caught in this country; I was sure he could help.

She declined, due to embarrassment, fear of the V.C., or

possibly due to fear of us. I don't know why, but she declined. I told her if she changed her mind, to please come through the checkpoint, and I'd make the arrangements to see the medic with as little attention drawn to her as possible.

After thinking it through that day, she stopped at the checkpoint on her way home. She told me she would like some help. I told her I would have the "Bac si" or doctor there in the morning.

Our medics were called on frequently to do things that were way beyond their responsibilities and also way beyond what they were trained to do. They were truly great people.

Doc looked at the teacher the next morning. When she took her hat off, I could see why she didn't want to be seen. The raw oozing sores were disgusting. He gave her a tube of ointment that he said he'd refill if needed.

It wasn't until a few weeks later that I had a chance to see the teacher again. When she saw me, she tilted her hat back to expose her face. She was fully recovered and was very pretty.

Because other Vietnamese were around us, we exchanged no words. She clasped her hands together in the traditional Buddhist gesture of thanks, and I smiled back. At least for this day, I could feel good about the war effort.

The other event took place at Checkpoint Four, but I was on Post Patrol at the time.

We had just delivered the noon meal to the checkpoint, when an old man on his bicycle approached. Lux went up to him, not because he could conceal anything, but because he'd stopped. Lux and the interpreter talked to the man for several minutes, and they kept turning to look down the road. After awhile they sent the old man on his way.

When he returned to us he said, "We've got a problem." Apparently a young, armed Viet Cong had flagged down the old man about a half mile up the road and told him he wanted to surrender, but he would only surrender to Americans.

Where he had flagged down the old man was enemy territory, or Indian territory as we called it. We radioed the base camp to see what we should do, and they told us to take our jeep and the checkpoint jeep and go pick him up. From their standpoint (coming from the safety of the base camp), it was a simple task. From our standpoint, it was anything but simple.

It was a given that Lux, Gary, and I would be heading into Indian territory. The interpreter would also be with us. We needed four more, and we let the infantry draw straws to see who the losers would be. When the eight of us gathered, we tossed around several plans before we settled on one we were comfortable with.

We decided we would travel, at top speed, to approximately two miles from the checkpoint. Since we had never been this far from the base camp, and weren't aware of the terrain, the lead jeep would pick a spot to stop. The spot would be the safest spot closest to where the old man had talked to the V.C. The jeeps would stop on opposite sides of the road, separated by twenty-five yards or more. Everyone would find cover along the road, except Gary, who would stay with the radio. The interpreter would yell for the V.C. to come out. We would give him a few minutes to show himself and surrender. If he didn't show himself, we would retreat immediately. In truth, we all thought we were being led into a trap.

The guys staying behind wished us luck, and we were off. The mini-operation was pulled off without a hitch. With thirty seconds to go on the time allotted him to surrender, a Viet Cong soldier answered our interpreter. He'd been hiding in the tall grass twenty yards from where we'd stopped our jeeps. The interpreter told him we would not mistreat him, and that he had to hurry. When he stepped out of the tall grass, it was like a nightmare that had come to life. It may sound strange, but you very seldom saw your enemy---alive that is. Most of the fighting that is done, is done at night, or with a very well hidden opponent. You shoot at the sound of someone shooting at you, or at a spot where tracers are coming from. But here, in broad daylight, was a Viet Cong soldier. Twenty-one years old, dressed in black V.C. pajamas, wearing Ho Chi Minh sandals, and carrying an AK-47. He had ammunition pouches across his chest, a canteen and hand grenades on his belt.

Since the interpreter and I were closest to him, we would disarm him. The interpreter took the AK-47, and I reached for the hand grenade on his belt. As I reached forward, the V.C grabbed my outstretched hand and pumped it furiously. I'm sure this was the first time he had shaken the hand of an American. As we shook hands, I removed his hand grenade with my free hand and began hustling him back to the jeeps. With a whistle we called everyone back, and were soon headed back to the checkpoint and safety.

Gary and I left everyone else at the checkpoint, and continued on to the base camp. We dropped our cheiu hoi off at military intelligence, and told him we would be back to check on him later.

That evening, we went back to the military intelligence hootch to see how the V.C. was doing. To tell the truth, we really wanted to have our picture taken with a live Viet Cong. After the picture was taken, Gary and I spent some time talking to the guys in military intelligence. The V.C. was being very cooperative. After hearing his story, it was understandable why he was helping us.

This young man of twenty-one had joined the Viet Cong when he was fourteen, not because he wanted to, but because he had to. The V.C. had come into his village seven years ago and rounded up all the young men. They then led them off into the jungle and a life of war. He had not seen his parents since.

First he transported supplies from Cambodia to fighting units in South Viet Nam. After packing supplies, he'd been trained to shoot the B-40 rocket. Throughout the previous three years, he'd been involved in many battles with Americans. After one particular battle, he found out his company of one hundred and twenty men and women were being pulled out of South Viet Nam for a short rest and recuperation. As they neared Cambodia, our B-52 bombers rained bombs down on them, killing all but four members of his company. He'd had it. He was burned out at twenty-one. He told his superiors he couldn't fight anymore. They then turned him back into a pack mule.

His job was hauling eighty pounds of rice from Cambodia into South Viet Nam. He was one of several hundred people hauling supplies at night, through the jungle, to waiting Viet Cong troops.

His entire life he'd been hungry, and now he had eighty pounds of rice strapped to his back. The temptation and hunger were too great. Each night he stole a handful of rice to add to his meager rations.

A few days before they reached their destination, a friend approached him and told him he had overheard several officers talking. They knew he was stealing rice, and were planning to execute him when they got to where they were going. He would serve as an example to the others.

All of those tortuous miles through the jungle had left him with time to think about his future. This latest information forced him to put his ideas into action.

The Americans were continuously flooding the country with chieu hoi pamphlets. The pamphlets encouraged V.C. to come over to the government of South Vietnam. There was a promise of reward for information and weapons. Most of the pamphlets became toilet paper, because the V.C. were afraid to be found with a pamphlet in their possession.

Our V.C. had hidden a pamphlet and was waiting for the opportunity to use it. The chieu hoi pamphlet was written in Vietnamese and English, but he was determined to surrender to Americans. He didn't trust the Vietnamese.

As soon as he thought everyone was asleep, he stole a bandoleer of ammunition, an AK-47, and a canteen of water. He kept heading in the direction the pack train was headed, knowing this would lead him deeper into South Vietnam. A massive search was organized to find him, but he managed to elude them. When he came to the road that led to our checkpoint, he had to make a decision on how to approach us. Wisely, he chose not to walk up to us.

He decided to hide in the elephant grass close to the road, waiting for an opportunity to flag someone down.

As he waited, two Viet Cong officers, dressed as civilians, rode bicycles by. They were discussing where they would look for him in Dau Tieng. They passed right through our checkpoint using fake identification cards.

Hearing this didn't make me feel too good. Later, when I mentioned this to Lux, who was manning the checkpoint, he said he remembered the two of them. He'd been suspicious of them because of their age and the time of day it was. They should have been in the army, or working, not riding bikes at mid-day. He'd let them through after searching them, because their cards were in order. They'd probably picked up weapons from the local V.C. once they arrived in Dau Tieng.

Our V.C. had waited patiently until the old man approached. He felt he could trust him to relay the information to us.

It must have been an agonizing few minutes for him as he watched his enemy barreling down the street toward him. After what he had been through in the last few days, and the last seven years, maybe that was relief I saw on his face when I "shook" hands with him.

Just because he'd surrendered to us didn't guarantee him a pleasant life. If his information proved valuable, and more importantly, trustworthy, he would become a Kit Carson Scout. Kit Carson Scouts were former V.C. that led American troops. They frequently saw things we didn't, and seemed to be able to tell Viet Cong from civilians. They weren't entirely trustworthy, but most did not want to get caught by their former friends.

Our V.C. was rewarded for the AK-47 and for the information he provided us with, but I'm afraid he will never be a short timer. He would spend the rest of his life looking over his shoulder. His safety with us was a temporary thing.

All of these events would happen at Checkpoint Four, but I should begin with my first week there.

My first week on Checkpoint Four was like everyone else's; long periods of time to think. As I waited on the road for my next "customer", I thought about food, my girlfriend, and home. I had managed to work myself into a blue mood and had decided it was time to shake it off. Look for the positive, a hard thing to do in this country. My eyes turned to something they would return to for many months to come. The Catholic church had a four foot cement wall across the front with a trellis gate. A beautiful red climbing rose bush twisted its way across the trellis. Besides the sunsets, that bush was the only beauty I ever saw in Vietnam. There were many interesting and unusual sights, but Vietnam was lacking in beauty. As I smelled the roses, I couldn't help but notice the bullet chipped wall it was climbing across.

The war started up every day at 3 p.m.; the V.C. would lob five to ten mortar rounds onto the base camp. They felt safe, knowing we couldn't shell their position in the rubber trees because of the rubber plantation workers. They would have free rein until our choppers got up in the air to pin point and attack their positions. The V.C. would lob five or six mortar rounds, and increasingly a 122 mm rocket, then hide until the choppers left. I couldn't help noticing and hearing the shells passing right over our checkpoint. The whirring, whistling, breath taking sound as the rounds passed over was unmistakable. The V.C. were launching their attacks from a quarter to a half mile from our checkpoint. At times, we could hear the round leave the mortar tube. It's a distinctive "phoomp" sound. When we heard that, we knew they were close.

After hearing this for a couple days, I suggested to Papa-San that we tie our checkpoint radio into a loudspeaker. We would act as an early warning device. Instead of running for the bunker after the first rounds hit the base camp, everyone would have a three to five second head start before they hit. In Vietnam, seconds determine life or death.

Within days the system was up and running. It worked perfectly, almost. The V.C. were so close we could hear the "phoomp" as the shells left the mortar tube. "Incoming,

incoming," was broadcast across the camp. We couldn't see them, but we could imagine all the G.I.'s sitting safely in their bunkers, laughing at their good fortune as shells exploded harmlessly outside. When we got back to base camp that night, we found out there were no injuries, other than the usual bumps and bruises. I finished out my week on the checkpoint and early warning system. My buddy Duc took over the following week. We called him Duc because the Vietnamese couldn't pronounce his real name, which was Lux. Lux always came out Duc, so it stuck.

About the fourth day on checkpoint, Duc heard the sound of mortars. He had just brought the microphone up to warn the camp, when the first shell landed on the checkpoint. The V.C. let us know they were on to us. They only dropped a few rounds, with very little damage, but no one was laughing. This attack was also their way of saying good-bye. From then on, the daylight mortar attacks would come from the north side of camp.

That still left us with snipers that would shoot at us as we left the checkpoint, but I came up with an idea on how to solve that problem too. The answer was an armored machine gun jeep. It could cover us as we retreated back to the base camp at night. Since the army didn't have one, we had to rely on G.I. ingenuity and theft. This project took a few weeks of planning and preparation.

During that time, I was asked to be the criminal investigator for the base camp. For the rest of October, I would be taken out of the squad rotation until a new investigator arrived to replace me. I got the job because I could type. Ten words a minute counted for something in the army. I thought I was in for a two week vacation, but was I wrong. We all knew the V.C. were the enemy, but at times we were our own worst enemy. The only advice I'd been given by the outgoing criminal investigator was, "Get the complainant to admit his stolen items were left 'unsecured', type up the report, file it, case closed." I couldn't believe my ears; that wasn't the way I would investigate a complaint.

I was true to my word for two days. There was a rash of petty thefts, all requiring reports that strained my typing skills. Every night, I typed by candlelight, in a bunker, until 3 a.m.. Missing watches, tape recorders, and money became a blur. Actually, they became "items left unsecured." Out of dozens of cases, only two cases really stood out, probably because they were the only ones I solved.

An officer in one of the infantry units stopped in to file a complaint about two missing pistols. I told him I'd stop that afternoon to investigate, and asked if he would have anyone involved or having knowledge of the crime at my disposal.

I arrived on the scene at 1 p.m. and was greeted by a private named Bell. Bell informed me that his captain had told him to gather everyone together in their hootch. He also asked if I would like a cup of iced tea. Since iced tea is not iced in Vietnam, I declined. I wanted to get this over with and get my "item left unsecured" report filed as quickly as possible.

I sat down on Bell's rack, with him to the right of me and three other guys on the rack across from me. We started with the usual questions: names, description of weapons stolen, when, where, and how. I was writing all of the information down, but was thinking "items left unsecured." When I finished writing, I jokingly said, "OK, who did it?" The G.I. across from me pointed at Bell and said, "He did." I looked at him dumbfounded. "Before you answer, I want to read you your

93

rights," I said. After I very properly read him his rights off my card, he said, "I want a lawyer." I once again looked at him dumbfounded and said, "Are you nuts? This is Vietnam; you can't have a lawyer. You have twenty-four hours to return the pistols to your Commanding Officer. I'll leave it up to him to decide your punishment. If I have to come back, I'll send you to Long Binh Jail." Nobody wanted to go to L.B.J., as it was affectionately called.

The pistols were returned, and my first case solved report went into the file.

The second solved case was solved as it was happening. I was returning from the north side of the camp, when a soldier flagged me down. "My Lieutenant sent me for the M.P.'s. You've got to come quick," he said. Without further explanation, I followed him to his company area. He was from an artillery unit close by.

As I approached a small gathering of men, I could hear shots from an M-16 being fired. Very quickly, the Lieutenant explained the situation as he understood it. Two of his platoon sergeants had gotten into an argument and had decided to duke it out after chow that evening They'd agreed to fight down by the ammo bunker.

The ammo bunker was a twenty foot by thirty foot, sand bagged storage area for artillery shells located in a small valley. We were standing on the hilltop looking down on what was going on. I would find out later that Sergeant Lopez had arrived at the fight scene first with his M-16. As Sergeant Johnson rounded the corner of the bunker, he saw the raised M-16 and ducked as the first shot was fired. He knew he'd never make it running up the hill, so he kept running around the bunker with Lopez in close pursuit About four shots had been fired by the time I arrived.

The Lieutenant said, "We have to stop them." I agreed, but I wasn't about to walk up to them. The only solution was to shoot the man with the weapon. I said, "These are your men. You have to shoot the one with the M-16 , and you have to do it in a hurry. Johnson can't keep guessing which corner he will come around much longer." The next time Lopez rounded the corner of the bunker, the lieutenant dropped him. It was a fairly serious chest wound, so we threw him in the back of the jeep and rushed him to the hospital. Case closed.

Those were two cases that were solved, but there were a few cases where I knew who the culprits were, but I didn't arrest them. I didn't arrest them because I was with them. You have to realize that the theft of army material isn't considered theft. It is considered scrounging, and is expected, and often sanctioned by those in charge.

Four cases stand out, and they will never be solved. We had decided to mount an operation that would make our bunkers stronger and safer. The 122 mm rockets now being used by Charlie made our bunkers obsolete, so we had to do something about it. The first step was to dig a hole and fill sandbags with the dirt we dug out. Step two was to build a framework of wood and surround the top three feet above ground with sandbags, about three feet thick. Step three called for a steel plate ceiling. This is where the scrounging comes in. The only place to get a four foot by eight foot piece of steel was to take it off the end of the runway at the airport. The original cement runway had been extended by piecing interlocking sheets of steel together. The engineer company wouldn't miss the farthest right hand corner of the runway, right? Wrong. I was called the very next day to investigate the loss. Being the ace detective I was, I noticed the perpetrator's mistake. The damp red clay under the steel was a different color than the surrounding dust. In fact, if you looked closely, you could follow the red boot prints of ten people struggling with a sheet of steel as they crossed the airport toward the M.P. company area. I informed the complainant that I would radio the Post Patrol, and we would follow up all leads. Case closed, and somewhat solved. After finishing the bunker, my thoughts turned to the armored car. Armor, steel; I had an idea. Three more trips to the airport, and we had our armor plating. We reasoned that, if you used that much of the runway, you were going to crash anyway.

Next, we needed a jeep. All of our jeeps were in constant use, so we had to scrounge one. It wasn't long, and I was investigating a jeep "left unsecured theft." We had to "rent" some welding equipment from a sergeant Papa-San knew in a tank unit. It would cost us ten bottles of whiskey, but we knew where to scrounge that.

Post Patrol entered the officers' club two hours after it closed and took nine bottles of whiskey and one bottle of vodka. Only officers were allowed whiskey, so they were our only option. The whiskey and vodka were exchanged that night for the welding equipment. The next day, as I was driving over to the officers' club to investigate a theft, Red, one of our good-old-boys from Georgia, was firing up the cutting torch.

I met a Major at the officers' club, and he proceeded to show me how the burglary took place. Little nicks on the window sill indicated entry through the window, which I duly noted on my investigative pad. I would've loved to have told him that the thieves had entered through the unlocked front doors, but he was having fun with his investigative powers.

As much fun as he was having playing detective, I knew he would never solve this case, and neither would I.

We had to experiment with the construction of the armored jeep in our spare time, but time would prove to be a crucial factor, very soon.

November, 1967

A new criminal investigator arrived in November, and relieved me for active duty. I worked the Main Gate for a few days, until I could be worked into the rotation. Since no Americans were allowed to leave the base camp, unless in convoy, it was a very boring job. The only bright spot in my very long day, was meeting Tran Ngoc Bich. Bic, as she was called, was a child of twelve, wise beyond her years. One of the unique features of my time in-country was the contact I had every day with Vietnamese. Most Americans in Vietnam never came in contact with the people, other than prostitutes and Viet Cong. I find it sad so many prejudices and hatreds were formed from such a limited amount of contact. There were certainVietnamese I hated, but then, that was also true for certain Americans. My hatred was a personal thing, not aimed at an entire race. Bic helped me understand the difficult position the innocent people of Vietnam had to survive daily. Her family lived in the second brick house from the base, on the street that led to the Michelin factory. Her father was employed by Michelin, so the house was a benefit, on top of two hundred dollars a year salary. Bic would soon make more money than her father, enough to send two sisters to the University of Saigon and provide a nice living for her family.

Our first meeting was an education for me. I was leaning

against a huge tree at Main Gate trying to stay out of the sun, when she walked past me on her way to the market. "Chou Co," I said, and she tilted her head in reply. She, like everyone, wore the cone shaped bamboo hat which covered most of her face, but I thought I could see the beginning of a smile.

An hour later, she returned from the market place with her sack. I bent at the waist in order to be at her level, and so I could see under her hat. In Vietnamese I said, "Hello, girl. How are you?" which wrapped up all the Vietnamese pleasantries I knew. When she gave her reply, I noticed she was missing a few front teeth. In my best ugly American English I said, "What happen you teeth?" as I pointed to my own teeth. She responded in very good English, "My mother did not tell me about brushing my teeth, and some of my first teeth rotted away." She said this as she brushed by me. There I stood, mouth gaping open in astonishment, bent over at the waist, staring into space.

A few minutes later I was back under the tree, contemplating what had just transpired, when I noticed Bic step out of her house and walk to the front steps of the house on the corner. I motioned for her to come closer, which she did, and I apologized for talking down to her. I then asked where she had learned English. She said she had been selling Coca-Cola to G.I.'s for about four years and just picked it up. Her English was liberally sprinkled with swear words, which confirmed for me that she was telling the truth. When I told her she shouldn't use some words she was using, she asked, "Why do G.I.'s use them?" I was trying to rationalize this by saying, "Young men away from home (and away from their mothers) sometimes do things they wouldn't do at home. It's not right, but it happens."

In that first meeting, we agreed to help one another

understand each other's customs and languages. She was a good student; I was pitiful. I did learn a lot, but I knew I would never be as fluent in Vietnamese as she was in English. I could listen and understand, but I couldn't get the right inflection in my voice to respond correctly. I tend to be a listener anyway, so I was satisfied. I found it amazing and helpful to hear what people would say when they thought you couldn't understand what was being said.

Bic sat on the opposite side of a huge tree as we talked. The tree formed the corner of a vine covered fence, so she was hidden from view. It wouldn't be safe for her to be seen associating with an American. The enemy had eyes everywhere.

I started bringing my dirty clothes to her for washing. I provided soap, and eventually, some more customers for her family's side business. Our friendship grew even after I returned to other duties. I managed to talk to her several times a day, and I was working on getting her a job on the base. Working for the Americans was the ultimate in jobs for a Vietnamese.

I knew our friendship had reached a new plateau when she warned me about Viet Cong in the village.

I was on jeep patrol of the base when I saw her walking back from the marketplace. We had just dropped the Main Gate guard off, when she tilted her head toward the tree. I knew she wanted to talk.

When I was in position, I heard her voice from behind the tree, "Do not go to the village today. Beau coup V.C. in the market place, very dangerous."

"Comb Biec," I said in Vietnamese, which means thank-you.

I immediately returned to base, knowing it would do no good to talk to our lieutenant. I went to the military intelligence lieutenant. I told him what I knew, and that I wouldn't divulge my source. I didn't want Bic placed in any more danger than she was already in. Military intelligence frequently did not live up to its name.

We got as many MP's together as we could, and surrounded the marketplace. Every morning villagers filled the marketplace to buy their daily supplies. Refrigeration had not reached this area of the world (except in our hootch). The marketplace was not only crowded with people, but every kind of live animal found in Vietnam. On normal days the market place was an exciting place to be. It was filled with sights, smells, and sounds that can't be found in the United States. As we filtered into the crowd, a new smell was added to the every day smell; it was the smell of fear---our own, as well as the V.C.'s. The tone of conversations changed as we started asking people for their identification cards.

With hundreds of people milling about, one gun shot would lead to mass hysteria, but at this point I was more afraid of a knife in the back. We tried to cover each other's backs, but that was difficult to do.

You can look into the eyes of your enemy and know he is your enemy, but proving it is hard to do. We arrested fifteen people for various reasons: ID's that were suspicious, excessive amounts of money, and some just because we could. People were often taken into custody to plant seeds of doubt amongst their comrades. Did he or she turn to the government side?

We took them in, and the South Vietnamese questioned them. Of the fifteen, three were kept for further "questioning."

That evening, as we were working on our armored car, we could hear the screams of the unfortunate three.

The next morning, as the prisoners were removed from

our P.O.W. compound, I couldn't help noticeing rope burns around their necks, as well as evidence of severe beatings. Captain Troung, the Vietnamese interrogator, was there to escort them to a Vietnamese prison, and he said lots of information was gained. Since I instigated the whole operation, I hoped he was telling the truth.

I had learned to never be present when Captain Troung interrogated a prisoner. Before I learned that lesson, I personally witnessed a military crank phone applied to various sensitive parts of the body, and, on one occasion, I saw him sink a bayonet through the back of a prisoner's hand. He pinned the man's hand to the desk top, which got results, but sickened me. I know the V.C. did the same, and worse, to our guys who were captured, but that didn't make it right.

That evening started out like most evenings. I found that routine added some stability to an unstable life. After duty I would sit in my lawn chair, open a beer, take off my shirt, loosen my boots, and write a letter to Laurie. I had to get it done before dark. I could shower and clean my rifle in the dark, but I couldn't write. The letters from Laurie gave me the will to go on.

I always started my letters to her the same way. Dear Laurie, I miss you and love you. I'm one day shorter, and nothing of importance happened today.

I had just begun my letter, when Papa-San came in and said, "The checkpoint is receiving fire and has requested reinforcements." This wasn't an unusual event. Frequently, snipers would fire at the guys at the checkpoint, as they prepared to leave. It was easier and safer for them to pull out if we gave them covering fire.

Everybody in my hootch responded by jumping into their jeeps. I slipped on my flak jacket without putting on a shirt, grabbed a bandoleer of ammo, and didn't bother to tie my boots. I wasn't too worried. I felt more excited than worried.

One hundred yards out the back gate, I was worried. There was more gunfire than usual. Instead of an occasional sniper round, I could place by sound, a heavy machine gun, several carbines and AK-47's. It was easy to distinguish the M-16's returning fire.

Papa-San ordered everyone to dismount and spread out. Gary and I dropped into a drainage ditch along the road. My mind was in fast forward now. As I tied my boots, I took inventory, flak jacket, helmet, M-16, 100 rounds of ammo, switchblade, and no hand grenades. My casualness in preparation could have cost me my life.

I glanced at Gary to see if he was any better prepared than I was. He wasn't. The only difference was that he had his .45 caliber pistol and three clips of ammo for it. I gave him a thumbs up show of false bravado and started forward.

As we got closer, the enemy machine gun was snapping off limbs in the bushes and trees growing on the top of the ditch we were in. Because of a two rut road that crossed the ditch, the V.C. couldn't shoot straight down the ditch. This was good for us, but meant that at some point we would have to cross the checkpoint road, to the ditch on the other side, to reach the guys at the checkpoint.

As was the custom, the check point guys had moved their jeeps onto the road prior to leaving. When I crossed the road, I used the jeeps as cover. Gary covered me as I crossed, and I used up a magazine covering him when he crossed.

We took up a position in an alley next to the Catholic school. The enemy machine gun was directly to our left, down the street. Approximately thirty Americans and one Vietnamese interpreter were spread out on both sides of the street in various defensive positions, and the sun had set. In the growing darkness, I saw three V.C. crawl across the alley too fast to shoot at.

"Papa-San, they're circling us on this side," I said.

"This side too," he said. "If they surround us in the dark, we're dead. They won't send a tank or reinforcements because they will think that's what the V.C. want. Everyone cease fire. Listen up. On the count of three, we jump into the jeeps and fly back to camp. Do we have drivers for all five jeeps? Sound off. Drivers remember, no lights, and keep your feet off the brakes. Don't give the V.C. a target. As soon as it's a little darker we'll move."

When he hit three, everyone was on the move. I dove into the back of the last jeep, others piled into and onto the jeep. I raised up to shoot, as the jeep was floored. To my surprise, I was staring into the wide, frightened eyes of our interpreter. I reached out, grabbed his hand, and literally ripped him off his feet on top of me. From under him, I could hear the whine of bullets and the breaking of glass.

No one touched the brakes until we were safely behind the gate in camp. The jeeps were in bad shape, but to our astonishment, no one was seriously injured.

What a night, I was alive, and I had a friend for life in our interpreter.

To finish my letter that night I went down into our bunker and wrote by candlelight.

Dear Laurie,

I love you, and miss you. I'm one day shorter, and nothing of importance happened today...

Since the camp commander was afraid of losing a tank to

a trap, the armored jeep became our top priority. Work would continue on it until it was finished.

We finished, or thought we had finished it, the next day. We decided to test it with a captured AK-47. When my buddy Gary fired at the armor, the bullet passed through and ricocheted around inside of the jeep. If anybody had been inside they would have been killed or wounded.

Back to the drawing board and the airport. We doubled the steel plating, but it was too top heavy. The jeep tipped over and had to be hoisted upright by a crane. Approximately one foot of steel was cut off the top to balance it. After painting, it looked very professional.

It must have caught the V.C. by surprise, because everything was very calm for a few days.

We hoped they wouldn't waste a rocket on our armored jeep, but we knew they would try to destroy it.

Two good things happened toward the end of November. Bic started working for us, and Thanksgiving came about. Bic would act as an interpreter and hootch girl. She would be one of many interpreters we employed. The others were South Vietnamese soldiers. She would increasingly play a bigger part in the war effort; Too big a part for someone her age. She would eventually have to stay on the base camp because of the danger her life was in. She would see her parents and sisters frequently, but always under the protection of G.I.'s.

A menu had been posted in the mess hall showing all the delicious food that would be served on Thanksgiving day. There would be turkey, mashed potatoes, squash, bread, corn and applesauce. Everyone looked forward to the best meal of the year.

On Thanksgiving Day, we lined up at the mess hall in

anticipation of a feast. As I got closer to the platters of food, I was nearly salivating. When I cast my eyes over the food, I was in shock. I didn't know you could get a Thanksgiving dinner from a can. It was a glorified c-ration meal. The only thing that didn't come out of a can was the Vietnamese rice.

As I sunk my teeth into my rolled pressed turkey, my thoughts turned toward home. I knew my family would be sitting down to a true, traditional Thanksgiving meal, minus the rice and minus me.

My next Thanksgiving meal would be in April when I went home. I was short!

December, 1967

When I think of December, my mind's eye pictures snow everywhere, not red dust everywhere. We were in the middle of the dry season now. If you stood on a dirt road, you stood ankle deep in red dust. The slightest hint of wind caused a blinding dust storm. Any place you sweat, which was every place, red dust stuck. Red dust filled every crevice in the environment and in humans. After a day on the road, your face felt like cement. Choppers were a constant source of irritation during the dry season. The dust they churned up could clog an M-16 in seconds. They were such a constant part of your everyday life that their absence made you feel uncomfortable. Their constant thumping sound was reassuring. Any abnormal sound from the engine was noticed by everyone on the ground.

Case in point was the day Gary and I watched a chopper crash. We had stopped under a tree we called the Koolibuck Tree to take a five minute nap. We did this a couple times a week. The tree was located on a hill near the Michelin Rubber Factory. We tried to catch a breath of cool air coming off the Saigon river which flowed below the hill. From our vantage point we could see for several miles We could see up and down river, across the flood plain to jungle a mile away, the bridge and water tower guards. Because of our vantage point and the other guards, we felt as safe as you can feel in Vietnam. We took turns sleeping and watching each others' backs. G.I's can sleep anywhere, anytime, and in any position. You may sleep light, but you have to sleep.

I had just drifted off to the drone of a distant chopper, enjoying the feel of a slight breeze on my sweaty face. My last thoughts were, "This is the life." You had to take joy where you found it.

I came instantly out of my sleep with the first backfire from the choppers engine. We picked it out, very high up and across the flood plain. The second backfire told us these people were in trouble. Gary was already turning the engine over, as I radioed for help. As I was talking to the desk sergeant, the rotors of the chopper stopped. It plummeted like a rock into the jungle.

The sergeant told us to secure a perimeter around the chopper and help anyone that might have survived. He would send more help as soon as possible. Gary and I looked at each other, probably much the way Custer's soldiers had looked at each other.

First of all, this was going to be a very small perimeter with just the two of us. Secondly, the chopper went down in Indian country. If we saw the chopper come down, so did Charlie. More than likely, we were all headed to the same spot.

We could not see where the chopper went down, but we could hear the ammo cooking off in the fire.

Gary, myself, and four others from another patrol, entered the jungle on a full run. The jungle soon put an end to that. Not only did we have to fight the jungle and heat, but we were soon separated from each other. I could hear people around me pushing through the jungle, but what kind of people were they? Not wanting to attract undue attention from the wrong people, no one communicated. We just plowed forward.

We only had to go a mile or a mile and a half to the crash site, but it took almost an hour and a half. The jungle tore at our clothing and skin, at times stopping us completely. I was at that point, struggling to pull myself forward, when I suddenly burst into an opening. The clearing had a small hut in the middle, with an old man laying in a hammock. He raised up on one arm as I burst into his secluded world. I don't know who was more surprised, me or him. I saw him look past me to see if there were any more crazy Americans out in the heat of the day or if I was the only one. Since I had the drop on him, he just laid there. There was no way to tell his politics, and I wasn't about to stick around, so I raised my hand to say, "Hi," and he did the same. I took off at a full run, down a small path leading away from the hut and in the direction I was headed. I didn't stay on the trail long because of the possibility of booby traps, and the chance I might meet someone. Since the ammo had stopped cooking off, I just followed my nose. I eventually made it to the crash site.

Three of my buddies were already there. We all looked the same---torn, tired, with perspiration soaked clothing and scratched skin. We had no radio, no water, and no food, but we were far better off than anyone in the chopper. All four on board were dead. If they hadn't been killed in the crash, the fire finished the job.

Eventually, all six of us were gathered at the crash site. Whenever fear is present, humans lower their voices, which meant we were down to a barely audible whisper. It didn't look like anything was salvageable, but the V.C. were geniuses at finding uses for junk. We decided to leave everything as it was, for two reasons. One, there were too few of us to stand guard, and, secondly, someone might want to investigate the crash site.

We settled into two man defensive positions, surrounding the site. We hardly had time for the jungle to settle back into its naturally noisy state, before choppers found us. We had no smoke grenades, so someone had to stand up and signal the choppers where we were. They could see the smoke from the burning chopper, but they needed to see an American. We took turns because no one likes to leave cover when a chopper noise filled the air. The reason being, you couldn't hear if someone was shooting at you. If you saw puffs of dust, you knew you were being fired at, but it could be too late by then.

The choppers lowered reinforcements in, and we were extracted. We were glad to get out. I wasn't looking forward to spending the night out there.

Only after our flight back to our jeeps, did I reflect on the fate of those in the chopper. I would later learn that one of those on board was a general. You couldn't help but feel sorry for those that died, but the thought that crossed all our minds was, "I'm glad it's you and not me." This was an embarrassing admission that wasn't discussed often, even though we all had felt this way at one time or another. This thought was probably the cause of survivor's guilt, something which all of us would struggle with for the rest of our lives. Our youthful feeling of immortality had long since disappeared, replaced by reality.

A few days after the crash, I received a Christmas tree at mail call. My Aunt Norma had sent a two foot tall, plastic Christmas tree. It looked like a green rocket with Christmas balls until you pulled the limbs out. It was beautiful, and heart warming, which is what Christmas is all about. Most G.I's had decorated trees, but they were banana trees with home made decorations. Ours was the only "real" Christmas tree. She really made a lot of people happy. My Uncle Ray, Norma's husband, had given me a special silver dollar before I'd left for Vietnam. He had carried it through the Pacific theater of World War II, for good luck. Someone else had carried it for good luck throughout the Korean War. I would carry it for 366 days (leap year), and it would bring luck to one more person in Vietnam. After I returned home I gave the silver dollar to my cousin's boyfriend who was just leaving the states for his tour of Vietnam. My Aunt and Uncle were special people and would always remain so.

As Christmas approached, enemy action was slowing down. This was a prelude to the truce that would be called during Christmas and New Year's. Since there wasn't much fighting going on, our spare time was used filling sand bags. About eight of us, and a Vietnamese interpreter named Phuc, were filling sand bags and drinking beer one afternoon. It was extremely hot, and we'd lost our shade, but we were still working. You could always count on the usual fooling around that comes naturally to teenagers trying to get out of work. If you turned your back, you could count on getting hit by a clod of red clay which would, in turn, stick to your sweaty back and eventually slide down into your pants. By 1500 hours we looked like red and white zebras.

Like all kids, we tired of that quickly and were looking about for something else to do. As luck would have it, a six foot snake slithered across the ground about twenty-five yards away. It slid into the military intelligence bunker which only had one way in and out.

As usual, we asked the interpreter if it was poisonous.

His answer was always yes; he hated snakes.

All nine of us started walking toward the bunker with mischievous anticipation. This was going to be fun for everyone except the snake.

Very carefully, we stuck our heads in the doorway and watched as the snake slithered around the floor. We soon came to the consensus that something had to be done. It was our duty.

Duc pulled his pistol and fired off a well aimed round, which missed. After covering our ears, and much arguing about his shooting ability, he let fly another round. Missed again. After everyone had their heads in position again, someone else fired twice at the luckiest snake in Southeast Asia. Oblivious to ricocheting bullets, several guys fired their pistols, all with the same effect. I hadn't pulled my pistol out because I was covering both ears with my hands, but decided it was time to show these "Girl Scouts" how to shoot. I was reaching for my pistol when out of the corner of my eye I saw the snub nosed barrel of a Thompson submachine gun. Phuc had leaned across the backs of everyone crammed in the doorway and snaked his weapon through the crowd.

I had just about covered my ears when he fired a full magazine into, and onto, the bunker. On a good day he couldn't hold the powerful tommy gun down. The tiny, half drunk, off balance soldier was totally out of control. Bullets, dust, and pieces of snake were everywhere. Miraculously, the only casualty was the "poisonous" snake, unless you counted those of us who couldn't hear and were covered with bits of snake.

As another day closed in Vietnam, Gary looked at me and said, "I'm short." I replied back, "I'm shorter." Neither one of us could hear the other because of the ringing in our ears, but we understood each other and smiled.

Christmas came and went, without the exchange of presents, snow, or good food. I was in the company of good friends, however.

At mail call I received a picture from home showing the way Christmas should be celebrated. My parents included pictures of them walking on the icebergs of Lake Michigan and other winter scenes. My entire body was covered with sweat, but my imagination placed me on the icebergs of home.

When I showed Bic my pictures, she was incredulous. At first she thought I was trying to trick her. She said, "No one could live in a place like this." Trying to explain snow to someone who had never seen snow or even seen a picture of snow was very difficult. The closest Vietnamese word to snow is ice. This brought the question, "Does it hurt when snow falls on you?" With sweat dripping off my nose, I tried to explain how beautiful it was.

In a few short months I would again try to explain to someone half a world away the oddities of nature as they gazed at pictures of Vietnam with unbelieving eyes. A picture may be worth a thousand words, but that isn't enough sometimes. You have to be there, and experience it to believe it.

On December 29, I turned twenty-one years old with as much fanfare as Christmas. Another day shorter is all it meant. That, and the fact I was still alive to see it.

To celebrate the end of the year, we'd decided to have a barbecue on New Year's Eve. Our menu would include water buffalo steaks, chicken, tomatoes, potatoes, pineapple, and beer.

The meat was grilling nicely, the beer was warm, and everyone was enjoying themselves, until Lieutenant Jones showed up.

He put a damper on the party by saying, "Since we have no ambush patrols out, I want everyone to be on standby. I want patrols of the base to be made until 0300 hours. I do not want any New Year's Eve parties to get out of hand."

Someone shouted out, "Just how do we patrol in the pitch dark?"

"I've assigned jeep patrols to different parts of the base. After dark you will have to walk to any disturbances," he said.

"Sounds like a good way to get shot, sir. Will you be out patrolling?" The implied message was understood by everyone, except the Lieutenant.

"No, I will man the radio tonight," he said.

After a very filling supper, we sat around shooting the bull until way after dark.

Because of the heat, we sat outside every night until we couldn't stay awake any longer. This was a special night so we tried to stay awake until midnight. We really didn't know what to expect, but anticipation was half the fun. I was on standby, so I felt sorry for the different Post Patrols sitting out there in the dark by themselves.

At one minute to twelve, a burst of M-16 rounds was fired into the dark, straight up into the night. The tracer rounds were beautiful. As if it was a signal, from all over the camp people started shooting into the sky. At its point, where all the tracers met, was a mass of red. The tracers formed a cone shaped hour glass in the sky.

The Lieutenant went nuts; he wanted arrests made. We could have helped him out, but we had all left our platoon area to join in the celebration. In the approximately five minutes of shooting I would say $10,000 of tax payers' money was shot up, literally shot up. New Years 1968 was off with a bang.

Not only was there not a single arrest made, but there were a tremendous number of requisition forms for more ammo from all of us.

January, 1968

The first week of January, my squad was assigned the most dangerous job we had to do in our rotation---roving Ambush Patrol. This job took us throughout the village of Dau Tieng. Our mission was to keep the V.C. from kidnapping young people, and to stop the V.C. tax collectors.

Even though this was dangerous duty, I felt good about what I was doing. The V.C would kidnap kids to haul supplies from Cambodia, work them until they couldn't work anymore, and then, frequently shoot them. If we could stop this from happening to one kid, then it was worth our effort.

To accomplish our mission, every night, one of our four squads would play cat and mouse with the V.C. Sometimes it was hard to tell who was the cat and who was the mouse. We would make our way from our base camp to the Vietnamese fort in Dau Tieng. We did this every night between ten p.m. and midnight. We would stay in the fort, drinking tea, playing cards, and napping until the American military advisor at the fort told us it was time to move out.

The squad usually consisted of twelve to fourteen of us. We carried a radio, one M-60 machine gun, one sawed off shotgun, one M-79 grenade launcher, M-16's and various pistols and knives. Everyone was dressed in tiger stripe camouflage, carrying only bandoleers of M-16 ammo and a belt of ammo for the machine gun. We traveled light because we were constantly moving. We didn't even carry water, because of the sloshing sound it made in our canteens. Dog tags were taped together for silence. If anybody asked, we were bad to the bone, until we stepped out of the fort into the pitch darkness.

Each and every one of us knew the village like the backs of our hands. I knew Dau Tieng better than my own hometown. I knew which houses were dangerous from an enemy standpoint, and which were dangerous because of the dogs they had, or even worse the geese they had.

We all knew the best hiding places and the most direct course to get to them. We all knew the best places to set up ambushes and to get ambushed.

We usually conferred with the Ambush Patrol from the previous week to see if there were any changes in the village we should be aware of, but because of New Year's Eve we didn't do this. This mistake presented me the most terrifying, helpless minute of my life.

Our first night out was a very hot, still night with a full moon. Because of the brightness of the full moon, we had to adjust our plan of attack for the night. If we were adjusting our plan, we knew the V.C would be doing the same thing. Because it was so easy to see, we decided to move to an ambush site and spend most of the night in one spot. The trick would be to get to that spot without stumbling into a V.C. ambush set for us.

After checking each other for anything that made noise or would shine from moonlight, we moved out of the fort. Because of the brightness we spaced ourselves about twenty feet apart and set out. We reached our designated ambush site without incident. It was located on the edge of the village, on the banks of the Saigon River. We hoped to catch someone on the river, but because of the full moon, we didn't really expect success.

The rule of combat was simple: anyone outside after dark would die. Everyone understood the rule; Shoot, and ask questions later.

Sometimes we'd stay out all night, but most of the time, we worked our way back to the fort before dawn. On this particular night, we'd told the military advisor we would return around 4:30 a.m. Just to be on the safe side, we never told anyone which way we would approach the fort or the password for the night. If we were at all suspicious of our counterparts in the Vietnamese Army, we would stay out until sunrise.

At 4:00 a.m. we decided to hat up. Duc took point, Gary took the rear, and the rest of us filled in the middle. We had decided to take the most direct route back to the fort. This route took us down the main street of Dau Tieng. We moved from doorway to doorway upon the signal from whomever was in front. Because of the moonlight, if you were at the front of the squad, you could see all the way to the end of the squad. The first person would give a hand signal to move forward if all appeared safe. In this way we hopped, skipped, and jumped down the street in relative safety. As I waited for the hand signal to move from the end of the line to the front, I scanned behind me and across the street at the roof tops and alleys covered by shadows. As I moved out into the street to start my jog forward, I felt like the moon was spotlighting me. I glanced at my buddies as I passed them and thought of these guys as my guardian angels. Angels in camouflage. I moved twenty yards in front of the first person before finding cover. I could see the walls of the fort approximately one hundred yards down the street. A feeling of relief was starting to creep over me. The night was almost over, and no one had gotten hurt.

The cover I had chosen was a house with a four foot cement wall around it. The courtyard, if you could call it that, was an opening of about ten feet by ten feet. As I crouched in the gate, I watched a man sleeping in a hammock in the doorway. Because of the heat, this was not unusual, and I had seen this many times before. I watched him for thirty seconds before I turned to signal my buddies. Still crouched down, I raised my left hand to give the move forward signal. Suddenly, I felt the barrel of a gun pushed into the base of my neck with such pressure, it forced me forward, off balance. My rifle barrel pushed into the dirt of the street. I heard, and felt through the barrel, the safety go off. Uncontrollable fear swept though my body. Of all the thoughts flashing through my mind, the only one I could act on was to ball my fist up to signal my buddies to stay where they were. At the same time, drool streamed uncontrollably out of my mouth, and my knees wouldn't function. For what seemed like an eternity, I sat frozen in place.

I honestly couldn't tell you how much time elapsed before I turned my head a little. My peripheral vision confirmed my worst fears. I could see a small man in the black pajamas the Viet Cong wore. He wore Ho Chi Minh sandals and cradled an AK-47. As I started to loosen the grip on my M-16, he almost, or it seemed to me, shouted,"G.I. number one." In this country all things good are number one and all things bad are number ten. I could have cried with joy.

My arm, still outstretched, and my fist, still in a very

shaky ball, changed to an all clear, move-out signal, all on its own.

As each one of my buddies passed, I saw their eyes widen as they looked at me and my new best friend. After everyone passed I struggled to my feet, waved good-bye, and stumbled off down the street. I made no attempt at concealing myself. As I moved forward, my only thought as I gazed at that beautiful moon was, I'm alive.

As we ate rice and drank tea we discussed what had happened. The military advisor said, "The house was a sanctuary for twelve former Viet Cong soldiers that had surrendered to the government. The program was called Chieu Hoi, or open arms. The former soldiers were rewarded for information and weapons brought in." He had told last week's Ambush Patrol about the new Chieu Hoi house, and he assumed they had passed this information on to us.

The second night of Ambush Patrol was a lot less hectic. The full moon was gone, and it was much darker. We used the dark to move around the village as we pleased. We had to stay close together, and stopped frequently to take head counts, but it was a rather slow night. About 4:30 a.m. we stopped to listen to sounds coming from the village. If you used your ears, you could tell a lot about where the V.C. were. Dogs barking, or geese making a racket let you know if the enemy was moving in a section of the town, or were sleeping that night. On this night they were sleeping. Since we were stopped, I suggested we visit the bakery on the way back to the fort.

Three bakers were the only people allowed to work at night in Dau Tieng. Their bakery was located on the main street, about one half mile from the fort. We didn't stop every night because the V.C. would get wise to that, but we did stop at least one night a week. Since the V.C. never tried to ambush us, I figured they owned the bakery, or taxed it heavily. We always approached from a different direction, and we always sat and listened to the night sounds before approaching the shop. Once we established that it was secure to approach, we formed a perimeter. Two men would enter the bakery to do the shopping. The only item they sold were foot long loaves of French bread for a penny. The shoppers would buy as much as they could carry, step out of the shop, wait until they got their night vision back, and then dispense their load amongst everyone of us. Usually, I would take three or four loaves. Because they were hot and smelled too good to resist, I would eat one loaf immediately. The smell of freshly baked bread reminded me of Sunday mornings at home. Dad always baked bread and rolls, and the smell would drift upstairs to where I was sleeping.

The smell always reminded me of my first roving Ambush Patrol and my first stop at the bakery. Like that night, I couldn't wait to eat it. My first bite was like heaven. The savory taste of hot bread can't be beat, and the somewhat crunchy raisins were a bonus. The other loaves were crammed into our sweat soaked fatigues, to be eaten the next day.

I had saved several cans of peanut butter and jelly from my C-rations, and was looking forward to a breakfast of peanut butter and jelly sandwichs. Before going to sleep that morning, I sliced open my bread, only to notice those crunchy raisins from the night before, weren't really crunchy raisins. "Duc, what are these black things in the bread?" I asked. He said, "Bugs---they get mixed in the dough; the bakers can't keep them out, and they don't taste bad." He was right, anything covered with peanut butter tastes pretty good.

These thoughts were just fleeting thoughts, soon replaced

by the euphoria that only fresh bread can give you. That euphoria was replaced by reality when the command to hat up came down by hand signal. Setting off down the dusty street, I couldn't help but laugh as G.I.'s passed me with loaves of bread sticking out of their pockets. Life was good, and I was short.

During my week on Ambush Patrol, we had six newbies join our platoon. Newbies were cherries, new guys in-country. They couldn't even utter the word short. Newbies was one of the kinder words used to describe them.

One of the newbies was named White. White was from Chicago, the inner city. I took him under my wing while everyone else ripped him because he had 350 days to go. We didn't know it then, but he was shorter than all of us.

I had decided to take him over to the PX to fill up on needed supplies, and asked him to drive the jeep. In an off-handed way he said he couldn't drive. "Living in Chicago, we never had a car," he said. His comment almost took my breath away. If he couldn't drive, he was of no use to us. You had to be able to drive. If he couldn't, he would be sent to the infantry. I tried to explain the seriousness of his situation, but being a newbie, he didn't grasp it.

I told him to forget the PX because we had more important things to do. I took him to the dirt road that ran along the southern perimeter of the base camp. I gave him a crash course on driving, no pun intended. He watched everything I did on the half mile of straight road. I then turned the jeep around, and we switched places. Very calmly, I told him what our plan of action would be. We would never leave second gear, or get above fifteen miles per hour. We would go straight, stop, and I would turn the jeep around. It seemed very clear to me, and I'm sure he was paying attention. I'm still not clear where my plan fell apart.

Drag racers would have been envious of the jump we made from standing still to fast forward. For some reason I will never understand, he started to turn the wheel. This caused us to swerve down a perfectly straight road. The first swerve just about threw me out of the jeep. I managed to catch one hand on the seat and one hand just below the window. With my butt hanging off the side of the jeep, I tried to pull myself in. I had just about gotten in, when he swerved again, putting me back in the same position.

As I was pulling myself in for the third time, I caught sight of someone leading a water buffalo down the road. As we flashed by them, I could see the very large rear end of the buffalo jumping off the road across a small ditch.

I was finally able to hit the ignition switch to shut the engine down. The Lord was once again looking over me. No one was hurt, but there *was* one angry little old lady who'd had to jump a ditch in front of one very frightened water buffalo. We weren't able to understand one word of her angry tirade, but we shook our heads and tried to apologize as best as we could.

She went on her way, still complaining to the very understanding water buffalo as we sat there trying to gain our composure. "I believe we've done enough driving for today. Maybe I can talk someone else into helping also," I said.

I had a few hours to calm down before our Ambush Patrol meeting, and I used the time to write Laurie. I tried to explain to her that I still hadn't heard whether or not I had received permission to go on R & R. I had applied for seven days of Rest and Recuperation leave in Hawaii about two months previously. As usual, the army was in no hurry. Laurie had already reserved tickets for the flight, and had made hotel reservations, even though we'd not heard if I was going to be there or not. At worst, one of us would enjoy Hawaii.

The date I had chosen was fast approaching. Even if I got permission in mail call tonight, I wouldn't have time to send her another letter before I left. Since I was so short, eighty-nine days, I wouldn't get another chance for R & R, and I needed it.

I still felt I would survive this ordeal called Vietnam, but there were days, hours, minutes, and seconds when I had my doubts. Tonight would be no exception.

We met the military advisor that night at the fort, and he said his sources had information that the V.C. were going to try to blow up the water tower at the Michelin Factory. The tower was a source of water, but, more importantly, it was an observation point for a full squad of soldiers. It was the highest point around for miles, and the V.C. wanted it eliminated. More and more, we were receiving military intelligence reports relating to the movement of large numbers of enemy soldiers. It was beginning to look like Tet, the lunar new year of 1968 would not be a normal celebration.

As a precaution, the advisor wanted to send one of his scouts along to interpret. The Vietnamese soldier came forward wearing flip flops, the shower sandals that make the flip flop noise when you walk.

All fourteen of us, in unison, looked at his feet. Even the newbies saw that this was unacceptable. He was sent back for jungle boots.

We had determined our course to the tower, and what each of our positions in line would be. I would pull up the rear with White. Pete would take point, Duc had a machine gun, and Gary, located in the middle of the line, had the radio. Duc and Gary also had newbies with them.

I checked my M-16 and White's rifle and we set off. It was approximately two miles to the tower. We would travel down back alleys to a pottery factory located fifty yards from the tower.

We had set up ambushes at the pottery factory before, but on the opposite side of the factory. The factory produced clay pots for the collecting of sap from the rubber trees. The south side of the factory overlooked a valley about the size of three football fields. It was a perfect ambush site. You laid in grass on top of a twenty foot wall, with a clear view of the whole valley. On this night we would lay in wait on the north side. We would set up amongst piles of small pots. We would be facing the approach to the water tower. The bridge guards would cover the other approach. We did not want to get caught in a crossfire, so everyone knew everyone else's position. No radios would be used, unless the ambush was sprung. Under no circumstance would the base call us. In some ambushes there were too many enemies to risk setting off the ambush, so you let them walk right through the ambush. You wouldn't want a radio message to alert the enemy as to where you were.

We had moved through town without incident and were about to enter the one half mile long alley that led to the factory. We had decided to move very slowly, and take frequent stops to make sure we weren't stepping into an enemy ambush. On one of these stops I had taken cover next to some cement steps that led into a house. The house, a Michelin worker's, was made of cement, as were all of the houses in this area of town.

As I took up position, I scanned the area from left to right and back. I signaled White to do the same thing. As I watched him, the door above me opened. In one motion, I clicked my safety off and put the barrel of my weapon into a woman's stomach. She was just throwing a pan of water out the door; it almost cost her her life. She was talking over her shoulder to someone in the room, so she never saw me. The light in their house took away our night vision, so we waited until it returned. I used the time to calm down. My breathing back to normal, my night vision back, and my camos soaked in sweat, we moved off down the alley.

Our final stop would be next to the small factory to listen one last time before moving into position for the night. Everyone had spread themselves out on either side of the alley. One unforeseen problem was a single low wattage light bulb on the side of the factory. It was located too high up on the building to unscrew, so we couldn't do anything about it. As I turned away from the light to cover our rear, I saw the silhouette of a man move to my left, back down the alley from where we had come. I then moved up the squad to the point position to tell Pete what I saw. It was determined that I would take two people off the rear of the squad and investigate. As I got back to the rear of the squad, I tapped White and Mark on the shoulder and signaled them to retrace our steps down the alley. Crouched over at the waist, with White in the middle, and Mark to the right of him, we had gone about fifteen yards when an explosion ripped apart the silence of the night. I don't think a nuclear explosion could have been louder. Someone had fired a single shot, or what I thought to be a single shot, at the three of us. To this day, I believe the shot came from ten feet in back of us. I believe I misjudged where the V.C was, and that he'd been hiding behind a three foot wide tree located on the edge of the alley. I would find out later that, from his point position, our Vietnamese scout had fired a shot through the whole squad. Pete would say later that he just raised his rifle and fired without a word. Maybe he could see a V.C. illuminated by the light bulb, or possibly he shot White. I don't know. All I know is, there was a terrible explosion. White's feet hit me in the head as he tumbled head over heals. As I hit the ground, because of the light coming from the bulb, I could see I was covered with his blood and chunks of his lung, . I figured if I could see it, the V.C. could see it, so I fired on automatic at the light bulb. Only one round fired, and then my M-16 jammed. That one round was enough. It chipped cement close enough to the light bulb to break it, and put us into the safety of darkness.

Thoughts were flashing through my head at a speed which, under normal circumstances would have led to utter confusion, now seemed quite clear and focused. I assume that is what adrenalin does to you.

As I lay there, I knew unjamming my rifle had to be my number one priority.

I had to help White, but not until the situation was under control. To approach him now might draw fire. I could hear him groaning softly and hear his breath gurgling from his lung. I knew he needed help, and he needed it soon.

I didn't know if the bullet had hit Mark as it passed through White, or if he was like me, thinking things through. I couldn't risk speaking to him; this also might draw fire.

I did not know what the rest of the squad was doing, but I knew they wouldn't approach us, for fear of us shooting them. Other thoughts of Laurie, my family, and home clouded the issue, but I was determined to survive.

I was scared, I knew that, but how much became apparent when I tried to unjam my rifle. M-16's, early in the war, were notorious for jamming. It tried to fire too fast for its mechanisms Because of this, everyone carried a cleaning rod to drive down the barrel. This pushed the empty shell casing out of the way of the incoming bullet. The company that made millions of dollars from the production of this weapon wasn't thinking about some poor soldier, lying on his back, trying to survive a few seconds longer, but at this moment, I sure was thinking about them. Thinking of them with a hatred that would burn in me for a long time to come.

I found the end of the barrel in the dark, but was shaking so severely I couldn't get the cleaning rod into the barrel. My only other weapon was a switchblade, which was useless, unless I wanted to commit suicide.

My only option was to crawl over to White and get his weapon. As I crawled toward him, I reached my hand out and felt his foot. Using his body as a shield, I slid toward his head. When I leaned over him, I found myself staring down the barrel of his pistol One painful twitch of his finger, and I wouldn't have to worry about another thing. Up to this point I'd everything I could to remain silent, but I was definitely reaching a point where I had to say something. If the V.C. couldn't hear my heart pounding in my throat and thundering in my ears, he surely wouldn't hear me whisper.

I chose my words carefully, so White would know I was an American. Within seconds I realized he didn't understand a thing I was saying. The drawing of his weapon was a reaction, or the result of his training. Very gently, I eased the weapon out of his hand.

With the weight of his weapon in my hand, the feeling of helplessness was lessened considerably. I had no idea how much time had passed since the first shot; it could have been seconds or hours. White needed help and couldn't wait much longer. I decided I would have to communicate with the rest of the squad. I would have to do this by talking to Pete at the point position. Taking a deep breath, I yelled out, "Pete, what is your status?" He returned with, "ARVN fired and then disappeared."

"Pete, radio in that we have a W.I.A. and need transport, now. After that, radio the tower and see if they can detect any movement in this area. Form a perimeter around my voice until help arrives," I said.

I could hear them crawling toward me, forming a circle as I worked on White. The bullet had entered his lower back and come out the top of his shoulder. We did what we could with the first aid packs we had, but we all knew it wasn't enough.

In a surprisingly short amount of time, we heard a jeep approaching with its lights out. Not wanting to get run over, we stood up and moved to the jeep. Two brave volunteers left the safety of the base camp to drive into who knows what. That says a lot about what we thought of each other. Most of the platoon didn't even know White; they just knew an American needed help. The first two guys who were asked found themselves, a short time later, driving down a very dark alley.

We placed White in the jeep, along with two of our squad to keep him from rolling around. The driver of the jeep was told to let the main gate guard know that we would be coming in, in about a half hour. The password would be Ferret, our radio call sign.

As we made our way back to the base camp, we couldn't help but wonder if, in the confusion, our jeep driving buddies might have forgotten to tell the gate guard we were coming in.

We took up position behind Bic's house and yelled Ferret. From the bunker came the response, "Approach."

"Eleven of us coming in," Pete said.

129

Once inside the wire, we all breathed a sigh of relief before we started talking. No one could verify who shot White, or what happened to the ARVN. We would try to figure it out in the daylight. For right now, White should be our main concern.

We all walked into the emergency area of the med-evac hospital where we saw White being prepped for a med-evac flight to Saigon, and eventually Japan, and home.

I know I was talking to a very drugged up soldier, but I had to let him know how sorry I was.

As I squeezed his hand I said, "If I screwed up by misjudging where the V.C. was, I apologize." At the same time, a doctor was trying to herd us out of his very clean hospital. If I were him, I wouldn't have wanted us in there either.

As we worked our way back to the hootch, I couldn't help thinking about the fact that I didn't even know his first name. He was called White, newbie, or something worse. All the tension of the night was wearing me down, and the adrenalin rush was gone. I felt like an old man at twenty-one. With tears in my eyes, I looked up at the stars and said, "Why Lord? Why White?" Once again, inches and seconds decided who walked away in this country. How long before I'm in the wrong place at the wrong time? Could I possibly stretch my luck another hundred days.

When I got back to the hootch, Papa-San met us to discuss once more what had happened. When we had finished he said, "By the way Mike, your R & R came through. You have to catch a chopper to Cu Chi tomorrow at noon." Panic struck, I had to let Laurie know what was happening. Thank God for adrenalin, because I was up and moving again. I ran over to the MARS station to call home. I had never used the radio to call home, because it was supposed to be used only for special occasions and emergencies, besides the lines of G.I.'s were too long. It was 0400 hours in the morning, and two soldiers were in line ahead of me. Both of them looked at me and must have thought I had an emergency, or maybe it was the way I smelled. Whatever the reason, I was moved to the front of the line.

The MARS station was a co-operative venture between the military and civilian ham radio operators in California. A soldier spoke into a radio, using radio protocol, to a very kind volunteer ham radio operator. He would then dial the number in the United States the soldier wished to reach. He then held the mouthpiece of the phone to the radio. The ham operator had to listen to the conversation so he could flip the receive or transmit switch when we finished a statement with "over". We were only allotted three minutes of conversation on the radio.

After the explanation on radio procedure, I was ready, except for one problem, I couldn't remember Laurie's phone number. Since time was at a premium, I gave the operator my home phone number.

It was 3:00 p.m. in Michigan when my mother picked up the phone. At the sound of my voice, my mother's tears started to flow. We forgot radio protocol, and the clock was running. I only had three minutes, so I had to take over. "Mom, tell Laurie I will be in Hawaii in four days. I don't know what day it is now, so I don't know what day I will arrive, or the time I will arrive. Just tell her four days from today. Check with people at Schofield Barracks in Hawaii on incoming flights. I believe there is only one flight a day from Vietnam. It will be an R & R flight. Did you understand everything? Over."

"Yes, over," she said.

"I love you all, and I'll see you in one hundred days. My

time is up on the radio. Over."

As I stepped out of the radio shack into the starlight, I thought, if she could have seen me standing here in my blood and sweat stained uniform, she might have thought that one hundred days is a lot longer than it sounds. I know that was what I was thinking.

As I walked back to my hootch, I thought I had covered all the bases. What could go wrong. My last fleeting thought as I collapsed onto my cot was, welcome to Vietnam, newbie.

The problems started as soon as I was cleaned up and ready to go. I was told I had to deliver a P.O.W. to the M.P's on the Cu Chi base. OK, no problem. I can do that. I'll catch a convoy in two days, from Cu Chi to Saigon, so I'll have time to deal with the prisoner. The hardest part of this trip I thought, would be getting off Dau Tieng base camp.

I picked up my prisoner and walked to the resupply pad where I was to await an incoming chopper. We arrived early because I was not about to miss this flight.

I ordered my hand cuffed prisoner to sit down on the ground. I tied his ankles with a short piece of rope I had taken along to tie him to the chopper. I sat a little way off, covering him with my M-16. Looking at my M-16 made me smile. How many Americans go on vacation with an M-16? As I gazed down the barrel at my target, I couldn't help but feel guilty. I don't know what the story was on this young Vietnamese, but I knew his future was bleak.

I couldn't help but compare the two of us, sitting in the sun, waiting for the same chopper. That chopper would bring me closer to home and my loved ones, and it would be taking him further from his home and loved ones. This flight was taking me to my future wife, and him to a prison or death.

Life wasn't fair, but that's the way it was.

As I was contemplating the differences in my traveling partner's life and mine, a soldier walked up and reinforced my theory on life by saying, "The chopper had mechanical problems and won't make it today." He obviously didn't know I had gone without a lot of sleep and was about to go on R & R. Even more importantly, he didn't take note of the loaded M-16 gradually turning in his direction, or possibly he did. My eyes may have flashed him a warning, because suddenly he said, "If you hurry you can catch a C-41 at the end of the runway."

I don't believe the V.C. knew why I untied his ankles and why we were running down the airstrip, but he knew I was serious when I said, "Mou lin, mou lin," and pointed my weapon first at him and then in the direction I wanted him to go.

The pilots of C-41's didn't like to spend much time on our base camp because of the fear of being mortared at anytime. They hardly ever shut their engines down. All their cargo was on pallets that a hi-lo could unload in a matter of minutes. Knowing all this made me prod my prisoner into a full run.

By the time I reached the plane, my uniform was drenched in sweat. I gave a passing thought to being overly tired and sweaty, but in the excitement of making it to the plane, I shrugged it off.

I tied my prisoner into the net seat on the side of the aircraft and prepared for take off. I knew he was scared. I could see it in his eyes. I'm sure he had never been off the ground in his entire life. Again, I couldn't help but compare each of us.

I, on the other hand, was happy to get off the ground. There was safety waiting way up in the air. Any danger of crashing was outweighed by the constant danger of remaining on the ground. He was experiencing flight for the first time. He was about to leave everything familiar to him behind. He was my enemy, but I felt sorry for him. I patted him on the knee, smiled, and pointed out the small window as we rolled down the runway. It was a flight of a little less than an hour, and he never took his eyes off the window.

The P.O.W. compound was located next to the airport runway on the Cu Chi base camp, so we walked there after landing. I turned him over to the guards and watched him walk into the barbed wire surrounded compound. Two thoughts about him will linger in my mind for the rest of my life. One was that I never knew his name. The other was, will he live to tell his children about the first time he flew into the clouds? Two nights ago I would have killed him without batting an eye, and he would have done the same to me. Today, I feel sorry for him. Maybe I did kill him by delivering him to the guards; I'll never know.

I was supposed to spend the rest of that day and the next on the Cu Chi base camp. I would catch a convoy to Saigon early the next morning. That was the plan; welcome to Vietnam.

I arrived at the company headquarters around 1100 hours, found a bunk, and started renewing old friendships.

At 1230 hours we walked over to the mess hall for chow. I picked up a tray for soldiers in transit and stood in line outside the mess hall. One second I was talking with friends, and the next I stood in sheer shock as I filled my pants. I've never had diarrhea come on so quickly, and without warning. I wasn't too embarrassed, because this had frequently happened to other guys due to bad food, malaria pills, or dysentery. The difference was, this time it happened to me.

As I walked robot-like to the shower, I hoped there

would be water. At Cu Chi, they hung empty bomb canisters over the shower stalls and filled them with water. They frequently ran out of water, often as you had just lathered up. I prayed for water, as hard as anyone ever lost in a desert. Not only was there water, it was warm from the noonday sun.

I changed into another pair of clean fatigues, but remained confused as to why it had happened. All I knew was that I couldn't let it happen (as if I had a choice) too often, because I would run out of clothes quickly.

I decided I wouldn't eat anything. Thinking like a soldier, I reasoned; no ammo, no shooting.

In theory, this sounded pretty good. In practice, it happened again as I headed out the door. Back to the shower and into my last set of fatigues.

I went to the latrine, just in case. I decided it would be better to wait there, than chance ruining my fatigues. I can't say it was a pleasant afternoon, but I made it through it.

I passed on supper and turned in early, hoping to beat whatever I was coming down with. The last week had been a rough one, and I figured I was exhausted. Exhaustion is a constant in Vietnam, so I hadn't paid much attention to it.

During the night someone woke me up. I had no idea who it was, but they said, "Are you all right? You're shaking like a leaf." I knew I was sick and getting worse by the minute. "Is the hospital in the same place it was a few months ago?" I asked. After finding out it was, I set out for it in the dark. It was only two or three hundred yards from our company area. About half way there I must have passed out, because the next thing I knew, the sun was shining on me. Even though I was shaking and feverish, I could see the red cross on the doors of the hospital in the distance. I managed to make it to the doors, but that was the last thing I remembered for awhile.

Twenty-four hours later, I came to in the general ward of the hospital. When I opened my eyes, a soldier in the next bunk was staring at me. "Yup, you're still alive. You've been out of it, for at least twenty-four hours," he said.

I felt like I had just been electrocuted. "Twenty-four hours! I have to get out of here," I yelled. A medic came over to my bunk and said, "You aren't going anywhere. You have dysentery."

I explained my situation, and he said he would get the doctor.

The doctor, a captain, after hearing my story said, "If your fever stays down for the next two hours, we'll let you go."

I've been in fire fights that seemed shorter than those two hours. I watched the seconds tick by knowing, one way or the other, I was leaving that hospital.

After checking my temperature, the Captain said he wasn't happy, but the food and relaxation would do me more good than staying in the hospital. He gave me a bottle of thick white medicine, with no label. "Take a gulp of this every two hours until it's gone," he said. "The only other order I have for you is to not over exert yourself."

"Yes sir! Thank you, sir," I said.

That order was ignored the second I passed through the doors of the hospital. I jogged back to the company area and quickly changed into my dress tropic uniform. I then jogged over to the staging area for the convoy to Saigon. I was lugging a suitcase and a carry-on bag, so I worked up quite a sweat. I also realized my fever was rising. If I die, I'll die in Hawaii, I thought with a smile.

The convoy trip to Saigon was quick and uneventful.

I was a little uneasy, because I didn't have a weapon. It was the first time in ten months that I was defenseless and felt like it.

I had no more than checked in at the Long Binh processing center, than we boarded transport for Ton Son Nuet airport.

As we were lined up to board the jet, M.P's searched our luggage and gave us instructions to put all carry-on bags into our suitcases and duffel bags.

I was pumped. I could not wait to sink into the airplane chair. For a while, I didn't think I was going to make it, but now I could relax. I must have taken my mind out of gear, because my medicine for dysentery was in my carry-on baggage, which was sitting in my suitcase in the belly of the jet.

I had just closed my eyes after liftoff, when I thought I'd better take a slug of medicine. I chuckled to myself thinking, I don't want an "accident" on this plane. Where would everyone go to get away from me. It wasn't quite so funny when I realized where my medicine was. An "accident" was a real possibility now.

The medicine had no name and was the consistency of barely liquid chalk. When I turned the bottle upside down to take my very carefully measured slug, it took forever to seep out. It was horrible, but it worked. I was in my last uniform, and my magic elixir was buried in the hold of the jet. This called for a plan.

The flight was eight hours to Hawaii, with stops at Guam and Wake Island. If I didn't eat or drink, and took precautionary trips to the bathroom, maybe I could make it.

My plan was working to perfection, but I knew that the medicine I had last taken was wearing off. I decided walking down the aisle was creating a strain on me physically, so I took the stewardess' seat. It was located three feet from the bathroom. When the stewardess saw me sitting in her seat, I mumbled one word, "Dysentery." "I understand. Good luck," she said. Obviously, she was a veteran of these flights and had run into others with the same problem.

My heart skipped a beat whenever I saw a soldier working his way down the aisle toward the bathroom. If two soldiers had to use the bathroom, I would jump into one of the two bathrooms and stay there until I thought the other bathroom was not in use. It wasn't the most relaxing flight I've ever had, but I'm happy to say it was uneventful.

I breathed a sigh of relief when I looked into the night and saw the lights of all the islands below. It had been awhile since I had seen lights at night or cars moving around with their lights on. "This might take a little getting used to," I said jokingly to the stewardess. I had no idea how accurate that statement would be.

A miracle had come true; Laurie was waiting for me at Schofield Barracks, home of the 25th Infantry Division. She had a lei to put around my neck and a hug that would have gone on much longer had I not had to find a bathroom.

After gathering up my luggage, and quickly taking a dose of medicine, I could finally relax. I had decided not to tell her about the last few weeks, or for that matter, about the last nine months. No good would come of it. We were here for R & R, rest and recuperation, and I needed rest immediately.

The first few days I slept away. I could finally let my guard down. I slept late, fell asleep early, and slept on the beach. I was cold most of the time, because of the difference in temperature between Hawaii and Vietnam.

When I wasn't sleeping, I watched people. I watched

them playing on the beach, eating at restaurants, walking around the zoo, sightseeing, and, in general, enjoying themselves. As the days went too quickly by, I realized I was not being very nice to Laurie. I was becoming angrier and angrier.

It had suddenly become apparent that not a person cared what was going on across the ocean. If I were killed next week, people would still come to Hawaii to enjoy themselves. The only people my death would effect would be Laurie and my family. Life would go on for everyone else, like nothing had happened.

At times I felt like standing up in a crowded restaurant and screaming at all these people enjoying themselves, "Don't you understand what life is like for all those young guys in Vietnam?" The sad fact is that they *didn't* understand. Part of the problem was of my own making. I had consciously chosen not to tell Laurie what was happening. No amount of mere words could explain Vietnam. You had to live it. A few minutes of T.V. news footage did not do justice to what was happening twenty-four hours a day in Vietnam.

Before I left the hospital, my weight was taken. I was shocked to learn that I had lost over forty-five pounds in nine months. How do you put into words the amount of stress a healthy twenty-one year old has gone through to cause him to lose forty-five pounds?

I don't know what I was expecting from civilians. I didn't want pity. I didn't need anyone to feel sorry for me, or my buddies. I guess it was my own frustration. I knew I was going back to Vietnam, and they would go back to their jobs, lost in the dreams of their vacation, and thinking about the next one. They probably didn't even appreciate all the little things that made up their very nice life. After Hawaii, I was going back to

Vietnam with a whole new attitude, being reacquainted with life as it should be.

I had eighty-nine days left in-country when I got back, and I was determined to make it. No more taking chances; no volunteering for anything. The infantry guys started a saying that was used by everyone in Vietnam, for every situation. "It don't mean nothing, nothing means nothing. It means nothing, even nothing means nothing." You could be talking about the weather or the death of a friend. "Put your time in and get out," was the prevailing attitude.

Before I knew it, my week in paradise was over. On my way to the airport, I kept mulling over in my mind how I would tell Laurie how sorry I was for my behavior. I wanted to know who would be waiting for me in eighty-nine days. I didn't deserve this wonderful person, especially after the way I'd acted during the last five days.

The only thing I could say was, "I'm sorry for the way I acted. I have a lot on my mind, and I know I'll be a different person the next time you see me."

We kissed, and I walked off to the plane. As I started climbing the steps to the airplane, I turned to wave one last good-bye. I don't think I've ever had a lonelier moment in my life; she was gone.

My entire flight time was spent planning my survival for the next eighty-nine days. A couple of other soldiers were doing the same thing, but they were doing it in Hawaii. They never showed up for the return flight to Vietnam. I wouldn't have done anything like that, but I *was* looking at all my options.

I felt I wouldn't have to worry about surviving the first week after I returned. The reason being, a peace truce would be in effect to celebrate the lunar new year, called Tet. I was actually looking forward to Tet, 1968. I should have heard the little voice saying, "This is Vietnam, short timer."

February, 1968

I arrived in Dau Tieng two days before the truce was to go into effect. In a sense it was good to be back. While I was gone, I'd worried about my squad. After taking a quick head count to myself, I gave a sigh of relief. Everyone was there.

It didn't take them long to fill me in on what had happened while I was gone. The usual G.I gripes: not enough beer, too hot, working too many hours, the Lieutenant was still a jerk, that kind of thing.

My real homecoming took place at the mess hall. As soon as I walked through the screen door, the Vietnamese kitchen help yelled out, "Co-nay, they say you die." My buddies had told them I died. I don't think they believed them, because they lied all the time, but just the same I said, "Thanks a lot, guys." Friendly bantering between the Vietnamese ladies and the guys went on constantly. Every meal was full of laughter and teasing. They would call us number ten G.I.'s, and we would call them Viet Cong (which some of them probably were).

The only one I didn't tease was Te. She was approximately thirty years old and married to a soldier from the

Vietnamese fort in town. She always had a smile for me, and she genuinely cared about me.

I felt sorry for her because she was Cambodian. Asians are the most prejudiced people I have ever met. They all hate each other, possibly because of centuries of war over land. The other girls ignored her because she was Cambodian. Under no stretch of the imagination could you call her attractive, but she had a warm smile, accented by one gold front tooth.

When she saw me she smiled and said, "Co-nay, beau coup kilo."

"That's right," I said. "Are you happy? I put on fifteen pounds while I was in Hawaii."

Three meals a day, when I ate in the mess hall, she piled the rice on my plate. "You eat, you eat, too skinny like snake," she said. Sometimes she would come out into the hall with an extra cup of rice after I was finished eating. It was quite often embarrassing because she would do it in front of all my buddies. You can imagine the ribbing I took from them when she would say, "You eat, you eat" and I would come back with "Yes, mom." She would frequently wave a finger in my face to go along with "You eat, you eat." If I started complaining in English she didn't understand, she unloaded on me in either Vietnamese or Cambodian. Either one, I knew it meant something like, "Don't you use that tone with me, young man." I'd heard it before on the other side of the world, and like there, it was easier to just eat the rice. Like I said, she cared about me. I knew my mother would have liked Te.

The day before Tet, Lux and I were on patrol in the village. Everyone was preparing for the holiday. You could smell food being prepared every where we went. Dancers, in snake and dragon heads, were weaving through the crowds of people. Firecrackers were being lit off by the hundreds. This made it pretty unnerving for us, but even more fun for the kids. Incense filled the air. Every home had incense burning by the front door and offerings to their ancestors piled up near by. You could feel the excitement in the air. This was, for most, the only fun they would have in an entire year.

About 1500 hours we were winding our way down an alley near the Michelin factory. We were working our way back to camp, because we had to lower the flag in front of brigade headquarters in a couple hours.

As we approached a group of party goers, we recognized several people. The province chief of Tri Tam and the mayor of Dau Tieng were throwing a party for their friends and families. We recognized the police chief, the local teacher, and other prominent members of Dau Tieng's upper crust. They also recognized us and immediately called us over to join in with their celebration. From the glazed look in their eyes, they had started celebrating early. The mayor poured us each a glass of some kind of alcohol, and we toasted the new year and everything else we could think of. As we were about to leave, the police chief pulled out a large bottle of clear liquid. A hush fell over the crowd as he poured his glass full. "Hi moui nam," he said, which I knew meant twenty-five. He then proceeded to drink one fourth of his drink. It must have been quite a feat because everyone watched in silence as he chugged it down. Someone else shouted out, "Nam moui" urging him to consume another half. The gauntlet must have been thrown down, because they all turned and looked at us.

Like I've said before, Lux could have been mayor of this town, and I believe he was starting his campaign when he shouted out, "Mout tram." The crowd, myself included, drew in our breath, because mout tram means one hundred, or the entire glass.

We both downed our glasses in one gulp, leaving the crowd stupefied. The "oohs" and "aahs" could be heard from everyone. We also found out what the clear liquid was. It was liquid hell. I could feel it burn its way down my throat, through my chest, and explode in my stomach.

More party goers arrived, and the story of our feat spread like wild fire. I started to hear the words 'souc mi,' and 'sou' which mean "never happen" and "lie." Lux must have heard them also, because he blurted out "Mout Tram." As the crush of people surrounded us to see this unbelievable feat of bravery, you could have heard a pin drop. I turned to look at his crooked smile and wasn't sure if his smile was really crooked, or if I was just seeing it that way. Whichever, he was smiling. The glasses were poured full, and everyone watched as we stared at them. Lux and I raised our glasses and said, "Happy Tet." I managed to hold it down, but knew one more sip would put a damper on the party; it was time to go.

If a vote had been held at that moment, Lux would have been the only American mayor in Vietnam; I know that for a fact. The crowd cleared a path as we stumbled to our jeep.

As we tried to gain our senses, two little girls ran up to us carrying our M-16s. We had left them laying next to the soon to be famous glasses.

Everyone cheered as we pulled away, probably amazed that we could walk, let alone drive a jeep.

The next few hours were a drunken blur. I know I have never, nor will ever, be that drunk again.

I did sober up a little at the flag lowering. Not that it was a sobering event; in fact, I couldn't quit laughing. I stood back, saluting, as Lux lowered the flag. Every time he looked up to see how much farther the flag had to go, his helmet fell off. The third time it happened, I was giggling so hard that I had to look to see if anyone else saw how funny it was. Over my right shoulder I saw a colonel and a major, and they didn't appear to see the humor in the matter. In fact, I didn't either, now. The fourth time his helmet fell, Lux looked back at me and just about choked when he saw who was standing in back of me. Wisely, he left the helmet on the ground and finished lowering the flag. I stepped forward, and we folded the flag as best as we could, considering.

On the way back to the hootch, we decided food might help us sober up, so we stopped at the mess hall. Te looked at me, and I knew immediately I was in trouble. "You, number ten soldier," she said. "You eat, you eat," rang in my ears. I knew I wouldn't be able to keep down her usual heaping amount of rice, but miraculously she didn't pile it on like usual. She did come out into the hall and slam down an empty canteen cup and pot of hot tea. "You drink, you drink, you number ten soldier," she said. I could only respond, "Yes, mom."

My Tet celebration came to an early end. With a splitting headache, I hit the sack early. All I wanted was peace and quiet for the entire night. I was not to get it.

About 0300 in the morning, the first mortar rounds slammed into the base camp, thus ending the truce agreed upon by all parties involved. Tet, 1968 would go down in the history books.

The first seven or eight rounds exploded in the rubber trees covering our hootch, doing considerable damage. I wouldn't know how much until much later, because after the first "crump" sound, I was in the bunker.

An impatient push from behind had rammed my forehead into the runway steel showing above the door. It left a gash that bled like all head wounds do, but that didn't bother me as much as the jarring my hung over head took. With every shell that landed, the more my hatred of the Viet Cong grew. My only solace was knowing the mortar attacks were never more than twenty rounds long. Wrong again, number ten soldier. The V.C. would usually drop from five to twenty rounds on the camp and then disappear before our reaction choppers got into the air.

We'd counted about nineteen and had started to relax. We always waited about five minutes, just in case they lobbed one in to catch us coming out of our holes. We hit twenty, and they kept on coming. Two hours later, we hit two hundred and stopped counting. We had far more serious things to talk about.

First of all, this was an all out attack. Were they trying to keep us pinned down, so they could breach the wire at some point around the camp? We didn't have a radio so we listened for small arms fire on the perimeter. There was random firing from nervous guards around the camp, but no heavy concentration of fire. We slowly came to the conclusion we would have to reinforce the bunker line. That meant we would have to leave the safety of our reinforced bunker and race across the runway to the nearest bunkers on the perimeter of the base camp. First, we would have to grab our boots, ammo, and weapons. We would leave to get our equipment, in twos and threes, as they walked the shells to the opposite side of the camp. We would then meet back in the bunker before setting out for the perimeter. After listening, we tried to pattern the incoming rounds. We determined there were four mortars, and they had quartered the base camp as their target. Our hootch was near the choppers, which hadn't left the ground because of the intensity of the incoming rounds. Our platoon area was taking a beating because of its location next to the choppers. The enemy wasn't interested in us; they wanted to keep the choppers out of action. We were just a bonus.

We came to the conclusion it would be suicide to cross the runway, so we very quickly decided to head south to the bunker line and then move west.

Mancuso, from New Jersey, had been hit in the inner thigh by a small piece of shrapnel, when the first round hit. There was an entry wound, but no exit wound. The hole was about one half inch wide and didn't appear life threatening, painful yes, but he would survive. What we couldn't know was that on entry, the burning piece of metal had traveled up his left leg and into his stomach. The razor sharp shrapnel had sliced some of his internal organs before it stopped. Mancuso was on his way home, but he didn't know it yet.

The first part of his journey began when we carried him across the street to the hospital. We wished him a hurried good luck, and we were out the door. We would have spent more time to say a better good bye if we had known we would never see him again.

As we approached the south side of the base camp, the small arms fire intensified. By sheer luck, good or bad, we had unknowingly reinforced the bunker line at the point of enemy attack. There were only eleven of us spread over four bunkers, but to the G.I's in those bunkers, we were an answer to their prayers.

I was carrying an M-60 machine gun, and two of my buddies carried ammo for me plus an M-79 grenade launcher and a pump shotgun. Between the eight of us, we pumped thousands of shells into the darkness. I should say seven of us, because the eighth person was loading magazines, bringing us fresh ammo, and manning the communication line connecting all the bunkers.

As the Viet Cong and North Vietnamese Army broke contact at dawn, we started to take stock of how much ammo we had left. In all the excitement, I hadn't even realized that the magazine loader was cussing in Vietnamese and was a female. As light gradually filled the bunker, I could make out a totally nude woman loading M-16 magazines as fast and as furiously as she could, the whole time condemning the V.C. to a life in the bowels of the earth and that was as kind as she would get.

"What in the world is she doing here?" I asked. One of the G.I.'s from the bunker said she was a prostitute and that she had crawled in through the wire before the attack. That was really unusual, not the crawling through endless strands of barb wire, but that she hadn't known about the attack. One of the first lessons you learned in Vietnam was to keep an eye on children and prostitutes. They always knew when an attack was imminent. I guessed I'd have to rethink my theory because this one definitely hadn't known about the attack. She was smart enough to realize that if our bunker was overrun, she would die along with us. For three days we stayed in that God forsaken bunker. It began to smell like my old football locker, where sweat went past the sweat stage and into the ammonia stage. We were resupplied with ammo, water, and a small amount of food, so life went on.

It wasn't a particularly fearful time. The attacks were more like feints, trying to feel out our weak spots, or just trying to hold us in position. I'm not saying we weren't scared, but this was the usual scare, not the mind numbing confusion that happened sometimes.

The base camp was mortared day and night the entire three days. Rocket propelled grenades (R.P.Gs) were fired, and a constant stream of green tracers entered the perimeter at some point throughout the night, but it just didn't seem like a serious attempt to   the camp.

On the third day we found out what was going on. As it turned out, we were not the focus of this Tet celebration, just participants. A country wide attack was being carried out in hopes of creating a general uprising amongst the South Vietnamese. From the Mekong Delta to the DMZ, the country was under attack. Tactically, it was a disaster; politically, it would eventually decide the fate of the war.

The Viet Cong and North Vietnamese Army managed to keep us pinned down for the three days, damage a lot of equipment, and scare the pants off a prostitute (no pun intended), but other than that, they accomplished little. They hadn't even been able to overrun the small A.R.V.N. fort in town. The fort suffered considerable damage, but they survived.

What they did accomplish was psychological. They didn't have the ability to attack and win, but they showed they had the ability to attack at will. The American media helped them turn the loss of thousands of their soldiers into a victory.

For the next few weeks our daily routine was upset. All of our time was spent repairing damaged hootches and scrounging new jeeps. We lost seven jeeps on the first day of Tet, to mortars. Any jeep left unattended was fair game. Everywhere we went, we carried tools to gather parts that were unattainable in any other legal way.

As usual, after further investigation, it was determined the property was left unsecured. Within a week we were up and running again. It was a good thing because we had a rash of jeep thefts to investigate.

When the mortar rounds hit the upper branches of the rubber trees, they exploded quite high off the ground. This probably saved many lives, but it wreaked havoc on our tin roof and our clothing.

The holes in the tin roof could be patched easily enough with the latex from the damaged rubber trees, but the clothing would be hard to replace. Some major trading and scrounging would have to be carried out. Until that was accomplished, you wore what you had, day in and day out. Since no resupply convoys would be coming into Dau Tieng for weeks because of the Tet attacks, everyone was in the same boat. The choppers that came in brought ammo and mail, just the essentials.

One benefit of the mortar attack was the loss of Lux's tape recorder. I say that because he had only one tape. At first we gathered around his bunk area for hours listening to Sam the Sham and the Pharaohs, over and over again. By the end of the week, everyone would cringe when he would flip the tape recorder on. As time went on, we went way beyond cringing, to the point of throwing boots his way. When everyone saw the shrapnel hole though the tape recorder, we all expressed our sorrow at his loss, but to a man, we all walked away with a smile on our faces. We all knew we would go to sleep that night without Sam the Sham and the Pharaohs.

About the third week of February, we had returned to normal, or as normal as things can be in Vietnam. We were back on patrol and running our checkpoints. Getting back on patrol in Dau Tieng brought about other benefits.

The ice maker in town had been put out of business by the V.C. The old lady that ran the ice plant told us the V.C. had taken parts of her machinery needed to make ice. She was probably the richest person in Dau Tieng, but she could not get the parts she needed to start up business again.

By acting as a middle man between the Americans and the ice maker, we ended up with new fatigues. Since only our platoon could be in town, we had a lock on the ice market. I'm not talking ice cubes, I'm talking three foot long blocks that are a foot square. Ice was priceless in this country.

We got the parts she needed, with the promise of ice which we would deliver. By the time we delivered the ice, it wasn't three feet long. We'd sawed it in half, using half ourselves or selling it, and trading the other half to a supply company for fatigues. Everyone was happy. The ice maker was back in business, lots of G.I.'s had cold beer, and we had new clothes. Life was good or as good as it could be considering the circumstances. Along with helping the ice maker (and ourselves), we tried to help, in any way we could, the soldiers rebuilding the Vietnamese fort. One day on our daily ice run, we stopped to talk to a soldier who had been on night patrol with us many times.

When asked if he needed anything, he said, in the small amount of English he knew, aided by hand gestures, that he needed a gas mask. The V.C had used gas the last time they attacked the fort and many had gotten sick. I told him I had an extra gas mask, and he could have it. It might take a few days, but I'd get it to him.

We received harassment mortars through all of February. Only five to ten rounds a day. The difference between January and February was that most of the rounds fell during the daylight hours. Many of the enemy rounds were duds, unexploded shells that had to be defused and stockpiled. In addition to the duds, there were a number of dud shells turned in for reward by Vietnamese kids. A lot of the kids made a large amount of money, in Vietnamese terms, returning duds. We had enough dud rounds to fill a large truck, and we had to destroy them soon. Our demolition guys would blow the whole pile up, out in no mans land, and we would provide security for them. Since we would drive right past the Vietnamese fort, I would drop the gas mask off as we went by. The plan was to blow up the duds during the first week of March. It was February 28; this being a leap year left one more day in February.

Gary and I were walking over to the mess hall for supper, the whole time discussing letters we had just received. As I entered the mess hall, Te saw me reading my letter. "Girlfriend write number ten soldier?" she asked.

"Yes, she did, and she loves me more than ever," I said. "Forty-three more days and a wakeup, and I'll be home. I'll say ciao Vietnam and ciao to mean mess hall girls."

"Oh, Co-nay you crazy. You eat, you eat," she said. I grabbed my tray of baked beans with my extra rice and moved into the dining hall. Gary and I had just laid our tray and helmets down when a 122mm rocket slammed into the mess hall. The 122mm was a six foot rocket that threw shrapnel two hundred yards. The noise coming in and the explosion were tremendous.

The rocket had ripped a gaping hole in the side of the mess hall. We used it to make a fast exit. I hadn't seen Gary in the dust and confusion, but I assumed he was headed for the same bunker I was. Half way to the bunker two things happened. I heard the sound of a second rocket screaming my way, and I collided with another guy. Although my focus was on where I was headed, I did see this guy running at an angle that would put him on a collision course with me. Our eyes locked for a split second and with that brief look, I knew he was not going to slow down. He must have seen the same look in my eyes, because we hit like two locomotives on the same track. It must have been God's will, as it was fortunate for both of us that we knocked each other down; the rocket hit not far from us.

Neither one of us were hit by shrapnel, so we each sprang to our feet and continued on. Ten feet from the bunker I heard the unmistakable scream of another rocket. I dove through the door as it exploded, and I rolled up against others in the bunker. As I tried to regain my breath, Gary said, "What took you so long?" I have no idea how he beat me, but what really surprised me was that Te was sitting next to him. Of course, she had to add her two cents. "Crazy Co-nay, you outside too long," she said. All I could say was, "Forty-three days and a wake up."

The third rocket was the last rocket. We walked back to the mess hall to retrieve our equipment. Sizzling in my beans was a three inch by two inch piece of razor sharp, red hot shrapnel. I ate my beans around it until it cooled enough to pick it up. After cleaning it off, I stuck it in my pocket for a souvenir. The piece came from the base of the massive rocket. It would make a good paper weight some day.

That night, before going to sleep, we all discussed where we were when we had our first encounter with a Russian 122 mm rocket. Not many could outdo Gary's and my story.

As I was drifting off to sleep, I thought how ironic it was for us, and quite natural, to discuss the rocket attack, while all over the United States young guys were talking about their encounters with girls and fast cars. Forty-two days!

I'm not sure I had fallen completely asleep when I heard the first "Crump" of mortars falling. As I ran for the bunker, I noticed they seemed further away than usual. Then I heard small arms fire in the distance. As we sat near the bunker, we all realized the Vietnamese fort was under attack. It was brief and vicious from the sound of it. We wouldn't know how vicious until morning because no one would leave our base camp to help. The attack could have been set up to lure us into an ambush. I'm afraid the ARVN's were on their own. At that thought I remembered the gas mask sitting at the end of my bunk. I would bring it first thing in the morning.

Gary and I grabbed a jeep at first light and went into town. As we approached the fort, we could see that quite a battle had been fought through the night. As is the custom after battles, bodies of enemy soldiers were laid out in a line for the whole community to see. Not wanting to run anyone down in the crowd, we slowly rolled to the main gate. As the ARVN guard waved us in, we noticed the fort was a beehive of activity. Everyone was involved in repairing the massive amounts of destruction. I spotted Long, the soldier to whom I was giving the gas mask. We were talking about the intensity of the fire fight, when I noticed Te's husband come out of a burned building carrying, what appeared to be, a charcoaled log. I called to him, happy to see he had survived. I'd started to get out of the jeep when it hit me. That wasn't a log; it was Te.

He gently dropped to his knees and laid his wife's body on the ground in front of him. I will never forget the look on his face, or seeing the object that had been my friend.

"Gary, get me out of here," I said. My feeling of sadness and revulsion was quickly being replaced with anger. I wanted to kill someone. As we again worked our way through the crowd, past the twenty or so dead V.C., I felt like jumping out and kicking the bodies. As we broke free of the crowd, I told Gary, "I need some fresh air. I feel like I can't breath."

"Have you forgotten where you are? There is no fresh air here," he said. He was right. There was only death, destruction, and the smell of rotting in the air.

"Let's go down to the bridge; maybe we can get a breeze off the river," I said. As I watched the sweat drip off my face into the brown murky water, I felt numb. I was emotionally drained. I would allow myself this time, and then I would have to snap back. Survival meant snapping back.

"You all right?" Gary asked.

"It don't mean nothing. Forty-one days and a wake up," I said. And I thought I meant it.

Surprisingly, Vietnam offered me hour after endless hour of time to think. In one year, I spent more time thinking than I did in all the years I spent in school. Considering my grades, that's not hard to believe. Many nights were spent with nothing to do, but watch and think. You think about everything imaginable. On my mind most of the time were Laurie and home. As situations became more tense, my thoughts easily turned toward religion. Vietnam was a religious experience for me. A very confusing religious experience, but a religious experience all the same. A religious experience that would affect me the rest of my life.

As a kid, I'd attended church and Sunday School, but I didn't like it. I wasn't patient enough to sit through a sermon, or to try and figure out what the Bible was saying. I couldn't sing, but I liked to listen to the hymns. I, instead, found God in nature. I spent hour after hour in the woods with my dog and

God. I wondered about everything in nature, and finally just accepted that God has a reason for everything; including my being in Vietnam.

Vietnam taught me patience. I could sit for hours and hours taking in every sight, sound, and smell, and being comfortable with just my thoughts for company. That ability made me a good soldier, and it allowed me to escape death on several occasions.

I knew I was a good soldier, but I didn't let it go to my head. I had seen many good soldiers and good people die. I accepted the fact that God had a plan for me, just as He had a plan for those people that died, and even for allowing some pretty evil people to live. At times it was confusing and heart wrenching. Trying to make sense of it just added to the confusion. It would have helped to have had just a peek at his plan, but I guess that is what it's all about, blind trust.

After Tet, when life became more precarious, I began to wonder and worry that His plan for me was to live a little longer and then die just before I was to be sent home. I was thinking about this one night as my squad spent the night waiting for our base camp to be attacked.

My squad and several others were the second line of defense against a force someone in military intelligence thought would overrun our perimeter. We were set up in a ditch which ran parallel to the airstrip. The idea being: if they penetrated the north side of the camp, our guys would fall back to our position, and the enemy would have to cross the vast openness of the airstrip. If they attacked from the south, we would just switch sides. If they attacked from the east, we were in a world of hurt.

It was an extremely hot, humid, and still night. You could tell everyone was nervous, because they were whispering to each other long before the sun set. The talking trailed off with the sunset to silence, leaving me once again with my thoughts.

With my chin resting on the butt of my M-60, I tried to rationalize what might happen and why. In my simple but sincere way, I prayed.

"Lord, I know the enemy may be praying to you at this very moment, and he may be asking for the same thing I am, but I'm asking for a moment of your time. I'm not asking for Charlie's life to be given up tonight, what will be, will be. What I'm asking for, and I will never ask for anything for myself ever again, is that you spare my squad and myself. Allow us to go home, and I will only ask that you benefit others from my prayers from now on. These are good boys, and they deserve a chance to go on with their lives. The V.C. and N.V.A. are probably just like us, just wishing this would all go away. It's all so confusing. Please give us a chance to help others in any way you see fit. After the boys in my squad get home, they're on their own. I'm just asking for your help to get them home. Just something to consider. Amen."

When you sit for hours with your private thoughts, they begin to sound like a conversation after awhile. It's really quite comforting.

I don't know if it was the prayers or what, but we all saw the sun come up in the morning. The enemy probed the perimeter at several spots, but they didn't launch a full scale attack that night. That attack would come a week later. The enemy paid heavily at the airstrip for that attack. My squad was still intact afterwards, and I was thankful.

A few weeks later I was tested on my promise of helping others.

About once a week the Catholic Chaplin, a captain, would come into our hootch and just talk with us. He was a great guy. He would sit and drink a beer with us, and most importantly listen to us, not talk at us.

On this particular night he had a request. Would we like to help him build a small chapel? He would get the materials and we, along with others, would provide the labor.

Every one of us said we would help as much as we could. Spare time and energy were equally scarce, but we would do what we could. We were all pretty excited. It almost seemed as if we all had made the same promise but had never told each other.

The Captain, true to his word, somehow found the material we needed. Actually, we helped with the lumber, which was very hard to come by. "Come by" isn't the proper term, probably. "Improperly placed" was the term we used when we had to explain its appearance to the Chaplain. To us, "improperly placed" was synonymous with "unsecured".

We had enough cement to make a pad that was fifteen feet by twenty feet. We had enough volunteers so that when someone set their hammer down to go on duty, someone else was there to pick it up. Work went on from dawn to dusk, and in no time it was finished. We were quite proud of our production. The chapel had a small steeple, and, contrary to most churches, a gun rack at the front door, and sand bags surrounding the first five feet of the exterior.

We finished at sunset and celebrated with a beer toast. This is probably unusual in the annals of church building history, but I felt good as I slipped off to sleep that night. It seemed as if I had just closed my eyes when the first mortar rounds jarred me awake. The first round landed within fifty yards of our hootch, so we all made it into the bunker in Olympic record setting time. As we sat there listening, we could tell Charlie was walking the rounds away from us. As we breathed a sigh of relief, we also heard the choppers cranking up to respond to the incoming shells. Charlie was dropping rounds on us at the rate of one every three or four seconds. Once the choppers got into the air, the rate of incoming would drop off. The muzzle flash could be seen from the air, and the choppers were there to respond with rockets.

Five or six choppers had gotten into the air when we heard one of them crash. From the sound, we gathered that it was less than a hundred yards from us. As we exited the bunker, we saw the fire, and heard the sound of the chopper's ammo cooking off. Everyone ran into the hootch, grabbed their flak jackets and steel pots, and sprinted off to see if they could help in any way.

As we approached the crash site, we stopped as one and stared. No one wanted to get killed from the choppers ammo and rockets that were firing off in every direction, but something more than that danger had stopped us. The chopper had come down directly on top of the chapel; it was gone.

We found out later that the chopper and a single mortar round had met in mid air. What are the chances of that happening? It did. The round exploded in the chopper blade, and it dropped fifty feet to the roof of the chapel. Fortunately, an infantryman was close to the site and was able to save all four of the crewmen before it was engulfed in flames. The two machine gunners were able to roll out and were dragged clear. The pilot was the most seriously hurt, both legs and both arms were broken, but he would recover.

When we found out there was nothing left for us to do,

we started back to our hootch, each of us lost in our own private thoughts. No one voiced it; in fact, no one voiced anything, but this had to be more than coincidence. There had to be a message, or purpose, for this happening, but what was it?

Was the chapel built to cushion the choppers fall? Maybe they would have been killed if they had hit the ground.

Was it something anyone of us had done?

It was just so confusing. In my bone-tired mind, I had to simplify things. The message I took away from the fire was, you don't need a building to practice your faith. You have to practice what is comfortable for you as an individual. If that means gathering with others of a like mind set, than do so. If you need a fancy church, or a humble basement, than that's what you need. If singing loudly or meditating by yourself is what is best for you, then do it. For me it means being alone, outside, night or day, in all seasons and every type of weather condition. I felt better now, as I continued walking with my friends. My simple mind had put some order and reason back into my life. I was wondering if I should ask the guys what they were thinking when Gary said, "It don't mean nothing." And Pete responded, "Nothing means nothing."

In the glowing light of another Vietnam dawn I said, "Yeah." As everyone trudged inside for a couple minutes of shut eye, I stayed outside and watched the sun come up. "It's gotta mean something, doesn't it?"

March, 1968

March came in like a lion. Mortars fell at about one in the morning. Not many, just enough to ruin a good night's sleep. Since we were all wide awake, and the danger seemed to be past, we tried to see how much damage had occurred.

In the moon light we could see a small crowd gathered on the runway, next to a chopper. Four or five of us joined the group gathered to see what was going on.

Laying on the ground was an 81mm mortar that had not exploded. A demolition sergeant had just arrived to disarm it or blow it in place if it was too dangerous to handle. Before attempting anything, he asked that we all gather around to shield the light from his flashlight. When we had gathered in a tight circle he assured us he would not endanger us; he just wanted to know what he had to deal with in the morning. Almost the very second the light from his small flashlight fell on the round, he said, "Um, looks like we're dealing with a time delayed fuse." None of us gathered were demolition experts, but we knew from what he said that the dud was not a dud and that it could explode at any second. That revelation must have hit everyone in that tightly gathered circle all at once, because we practically knocked each other down in our haste to get as far away as possible from this fool and his ridiculous job. From a very safe distance, we could hear him laughing uproariously.

We had three sergeants who were in charge of dismantling unexploded shells. All three were friendly, very nervous, and drank heavily. Since we were the only Americans allowed off base, we were frequently approached by the locals about rewards for duds, and all too often the duds were given to us. Because of this, we dealt with the demo sergeants on a daily basis. We often provided security for them as they dismantled mines, bombs, shells, and hand grenades. It was easy to understand why they were nervous and easier to understand why they drank so much.

Because of Tet and the constant barrage of mortars and rockets through all of February, the sergeants had accumulated a mound of ordinance that had to be destroyed. Just because they were defused did not mean they were safe to have around.

A request was made by the demo nuts for us to provide security for them while they destroyed the duds. The pile was so large it would have to be destroyed off the base camp. This meant we would have to load a large truck with the explosives and transport it out past Checkpoint Four to no man's land, unload it, and detonate the pile. After detonation we would have to go back and make sure everything was destroyed. We didn't want the V.C. to get their little treasures back.

The loading went very well. The demo sergeants laughed at our nervousness and occasionally threw things at us that we hoped would not explode. During the loading process they would suddenly scream, "Don't move!" Of course, they would wait until you had just picked up a large round of ammunition and then roar with laughter. Like I said, sick people, very sick people.

We drew straws to see which of us would have to drive the truck. I won; Gary lost. He climbed into the truck and slowly drove off with the rest of us either leading or following at a great distance.

Approximately one half hour later we reached Checkpoint Four. After telling our guys what we were about to do, and getting the ARVN's to understand what was about to happen, we moved out into no man's land. No man's land is a misnomer. There were people out there using the road, but no one could step off the raised road or they would be shot.

Outward from the checkpoint the jungle had been cleared for one to two miles creating an open field of fire. The road running through the middle was raised about ten feet from the surrounding area. The road was a link with distant villages and Dau Tieng. As far as a bullet could travel was considered no man's land. Use the road, but don't make the mistake of getting off the road.

Since we had just spoken to the people that make it a no man's land, we proceeded about one mile into it. We stopped at a point where we felt relatively safe from the V.C. shooting us from the jungle opposite our checkpoint. As soon as we secured the area and set up a perimeter, we began unloading the explosives. We took turns unloading the truck and completed the job quickly.

A block of C-4 plastic explosive was placed in the middle of the pile, with a six foot fuse sticking out. The fuse was long enough to allow us plenty of time to return to the checkpoint.

We parked our vehicles on the road knowing we

wouldn't block traffic because there wasn't any. The only time the road was used was in the morning when distant villagers came to the market in Dau Tieng.

We were gathered in a group talking when an ARVN soldier on the top floor of the bunker yelled down to us. I picked up some of what he was saying, but it all became clear when I followed his pointing finger. "Oh, my God, here comes an ox cart," I said. Way off in the distance, a large wheeled cart, drawn by an ox, was slowly walking our way. As one, we began shouting in English and Vietnamese, "Go back, stop." The old man on the cart appeared to be sleeping, and the ox kept pulling him closer and closer to our pile of explosives. Since the pile was out of sight below the road, we weren't sure where it was, but we knew he had to be close to it. One of the ARVN's in the bunker let loose a burst of automatic fire over the farmer's head. As with anyone, it got his attention. He stopped dead in his tracks and appeared to be trying to figure out what he had done wrong. It didn't take long to get his answer. The explosion was tremendous. The farmer and his cart disappeared in the dust and smoke.

We ran for our jeeps and tore down the road, afraid of what we would find when we got there. What we found was an ox laying on its side, an overturned cart, and a farmer trying to unplug his ears. We all breathed a sigh of relief when we found him unharmed. The concussion had knocked him and his cart over, but he was not touched by any shrapnel. The force had rolled him down the embankment on the opposite side of the road. Besides temporarily losing his hearing and getting very dirty, he was fine.

The farmer explained to one of the ARVN's that this had been quite a day. He had broken a wheel, and that's why he was so late getting to town. He had missed his chance to sell at the market place, so he would have to spend the night in Dau Tieng, and sell his pineapples in the morning before returning home. Lastly, he had met us.

We decided that the rest of his day was about to get a lot better. We helped him right his cart, and gave him ten dollars in piasters. That was more than he'd make in a month or two. I'm not sure he could hear our sincere apologies, but the money sent him on his way smiling.

You would think we'd have learned to expect the unexpected, but once again it was a lesson learned. For me, that lesson was, don't ever associate with those reckless demolition men again. Within a week those words would come back to haunt me.

Since Tet, we had to be extra diligent in our security measures, which on this morning, meant protecting our checkpoint people as they got into place for the day. For some odd reason I will never understand, I drove the jeep. Wicklow took the machine gun, and Pete rode shotgun. Ninety-nine percent of the time I was the machine gunner, but on this day I drove.

We were on our way toward the checkpoint by first light. Everyday was like the next: clear blue sky, cool until the sun came up, then hot and humid. Cool meant 85 degrees, and hot meant 100-115 degrees. Any day now the first rains of the monsoon season would start. Everyone was looking forward to the drenching rains. We had forgotten how miserable it was to be constantly wet. All we thought about was settling the six inches of dust that covered the ground and everything else.

I was thinking about the weather because my job this morning was to provide security on the dirt road next to

Checkpoint Three as our guys moved into the bunkers.

The V.C. had gotten into the bunkers to ambush us and had planted mines on several occasions since Tet, so we were very cautious. One factor working in our favor was a spy. We paid a man and his son to watch our bunkers every night. He and his son watched from across the street by the church. If anything suspicious happened during the night, he turned a flower pot upside down on the wall next to the school. As we approached the checkpoint we would check the flower pot, but we still approached with caution. The spy was helpful, but you couldn't completely trust anyone or anything in this country.

Mostly we had to deal with mines and booby traps, but on one occasion five V.C. were trapped and killed in our bunkers. We were prepared for them, all because of the flower pot spy.

As everyone else was pulling in around the bunker, Wick, Pete, and I pulled onto the dirt road that ran north along the rubber trees. Our job was to provide a crossfire on anyone who might shoot from the rubber trees. We were approximately one hundred yards from everyone else, watching them and watching the forest of rubber trees.

The road, if you could call it a road, was bordered on one side by a six foot deep ditch and on the other side by long rolls of concertina barb wire. The rolls of barb wire were piled three high and ran for about one mile along the rubber trees. The road was dirt and only wide enough for one vehicle.

Wick stayed with the machine gun while Pete and I spread out away from the jeep. Wick suddenly yelled to us, "Let's hat up. The other jeeps are returning to the base camp." Since our jeep was facing north, we decided to continue down the road where it joined another road that would return us to the base camp. We could have backed up one hundred yards to the main road, but we did that yesterday. In all, we would drive two hundred yards further, but that seemed reasonable. There was no place to turn the jeep around, so off we went. Since we were all veterans of this procedure, we knew what was expected of us. I was driving; My area of concentration was down the road. Pete was riding shotgun; His area was beyond the barbed wire, into the forest. Since the left side of the road was a ditch and an open field, Wick covered the trees to the right and our rear.

As usual, we traveled at high rates of speed. The only thing that aroused my curiosity was a small branch laying in the road straight ahead. Since the rubber trees hung over the road, the branch shouldn't be unusual, but it was. In the few seconds it took to reach the branch, I had noted no other branches around and had remembered that the wind was dead still during the night. The usual was unusual. Almost subconsciously, I edged as close to the barb wire as I could. As we bore down on the cluster of leaves, I noticed one bare stick protruding out of the cluster. I missed the cluster of leaves by about three or four inches. As I passed it, I looked straight down into it and thought I had seen some metal. I stopped twenty yards past the branch and started walking back to it. "What are you doing?" Pete asked. "Something is not right. Cover the woods. I'll just be a minute," I said. As I stood over the branch, I knew immediately what I was dealing with. Very carefully, I lifted the branch straight up. What remained was the stick with a metal ring at its base. "You guys owe me a beer. We just missed a tilt rod mine," I said. The stick was supposed to have been hit by our bumper. Once it had tilted fifteen degrees off center, it would have triggered the mine. Very carefully, we scraped away the dirt, exposing an antitank mine. If we had hit the mine, they would never have found enough of us to put in a body bag. This was a very large mine.

Now, we were faced with a dilemma. We didn't want to dig it up because the V.C. would occasionally put one mine under the other. When you lifted one, the other exploded. That, plus the fact I had decided to have as little to do with our demolition team as possible, caused us to take care of the mine ourselves.

Wick said, "Let's throw a grenade at it." Being a grenade man myself, and always having one or two along with me, it sounded like a good idea. My first effort bounced on the hard road and rolled off before exploding. My last grenade was wasted by Wick, the guy who couldn't understand how I missed.

Our next idea, the only idea we told people about, was to tie a string to the stick and from a distance, pull the string. The only problem was we had no string. Pete said, "The checkpoint has extra commo wire; I'll go get some."

"Get about twenty yards," Wick yelled after him. Remembering the incident with the farmer, I yelled, "Get forty yards."

When Pete returned with the wire, we tied a loop in one end and stretched the wire as far away as it would go. We then dropped the loop over the stick and ran back to the other end. We dropped down in the ditch, yelled, "Fire in the hole," and pulled the wire. I wasn't prepared for the extent of the explosion. A large section of the road rose up through the trees, taking most of the trees' leaves with it. Leaves, dirt, rocks, and branches rained down on us as we huddled in the ditch. I was beginning to think we might fit right in with our demolition team. After seeing the hole in the road, I knew we would fit right in.

The hole was approximately three feet deep and five feet across. Needless to say, no one would be using this road for awhile. We actually thought about filling the hole in, but we had no shovels, and the dirt from the hole was spread over a very large area. "Oh well, our work here is done. Let's move on to our next adventure," said Pete.

Actually, Pete wasn't joking; the next adventure was always close to happening at any moment. Because of Tet, and increasing Viet Cong and N.V.A. activity, we had a very interesting March. My squad spent a lot of time on night patrol. The V.C were trying to kidnap young kids to replenish the supplies they had used up in their Tet attacks. They were also trying to collect taxes from people who had nothing left to give. Our job was to stop them, and we were determined. Our determination paid off on many occasions, with results that made everyone happy, excluding the V.C. As with everything in life, you can't win all the time. Those times tend to be the most bizarre.

One of those bizarre events began like most night patrols began, at the Vietnamese fort in Dau Tieng. Our mission would involve limited movement, because it was a very dark night. There was no moonlight, and the stars were covered by clouds. In other words: you couldn't see your hand in front of your face.

We decided to set up an ambush where three roads and two alleys all came together, approximately a half mile from the fort. After we covered the entire mission and checked each other for camouflage or noise problems, we moved to the gate of the fort. Gary radioed the base camp that we were about to move out, "Ferret one, this is Ferret six, clear for the night."

"Ferret six, this is Ferret one, hold. Do you read?" came the reply no one wanted to hear. "We read you loud and clear, and holding," Gary said, as we all gathered around the radio. "This isn't good, somewhere, somehow, someone has heard something. Since we're the only ones out here, it has to be the bridge or water tower guards," I said. "If that's true, they're going to want us to patrol the area between us and them," Pete said. That meant fourteen guys moving in the pitch dark about two miles further than we had planned. We all sat in silence knowing that was not good. Almost as a sign from God, the first rains of the new monsoon season started to fall. We had all waited for months in anticipation of the first rains, but why now? Just enough rain fell to soak us through.

"Ferret six, this is one. Movement has been observed on the river, south of the bridge. Adjust your mission as needed. Do you copy?"

"Ferret one, this is six, copied and out," said Gary. For the next fifteen minutes we all discussed the pros and cons of this mission. This was a military unit, but we were all friends and veterans also. Each of us contributed valuable information that one person might have overlooked. We all knew what was expected of us and would carry out the mission.

"Let's hat up," said Lux, as he took point and started off with the rest of us falling in behind him. I pulled up the rear, glancing over my shoulder at the friendly confines of the fort with mixed feelings. Part of me wanted to return, and part of me really wanted to move out into the darkness. It didn't really matter what I thought. I didn't have a choice.

A few steps down the road, I had cleared my mind of everything that could hinder my survival. I was totally in tune with my surroundings and ignored the discomfort of wet clothes. My weapon was an extension of me. It and I were one. My alertness and powers of concentration were at their highest level.

The adrenalin was kicking in.

I couldn't see Lux on point; I could barely see the man three feet in front of me, but I trusted he was doing his job, just as he trusted I was doing mine. We had to trust each other, and no one else.

We had moved about a half mile when we heard dogs barking. The barking was coming from the direction we were headed. The adrenalin started pumping by the pint.

As we approached our original ambush point, the corner with the alleys coming out to the road, we stopped to listen before crossing the street. We sat in place for fifteen minutes or more because no one wanted to enter the alley.

The alley was one we often avoided on a normal night. It led from the street, past a few stores, and on to a few huts. Once past the huts, the alley narrowed and was bordered by a thick bamboo forest on each side of the alley.

The bamboo trees made a cave out of the alley. It was dark and spooky during the day. We avoided Bamboo Alley whenever we could.

Word came down the line that we were moving out. The entire squad crossed the street without incident. We regrouped on the opposite side of the street, and again listened for anything suspicious. After a five minute stop, Lux once more set out. I had just passed the last store and was thinking that Lux must be about to enter Bamboo Alley, when the clanging crash of metal broke the stillness of the night. At night, in this type of situation, any noise seems loud, but this gripped my heart like a hand. Everyone froze in place, the adrenalin pumping by the quart through our veins. Word was sent back to retreat to the street where we would regroup and rethink our position. When we'd formed a perimeter and felt as secure as we could feel, Lux told us what had happened. "I had just entered the alley and was moving my arm slowly up and down, feeling for   trip wires, when my foot kicked a can that had been placed in the path." The V.C. had placed cans across the entire path so they knew exactly where we were, and where we had intended to go. I say intended, because it would be suicide to move down that alley now.

Since we had given away our position, we decided to radio the base camp and alert them to our situation. Gary gave them a very vivid account of what had happened, but they didn't seem to grasp the seriousness of the situation. We were told to proceed with our mission. We all knew that Lieutenant Jones had made that decision.

"Once more, into the breach," said Gary. "Heard that in a history class once, never fully understood it, but I do now."

We formed our line of march once again and prepared to move out. A chopper was approaching. We waited for it to fly over, so it wouldn't ruin our ability to hear. As it got above us, it lit us up with a flood light. They must have had a starlight on board, or they were told to light up a certain area of the town. Whatever the reason, we were bathed in light, wondering who would shoot us first: the chopper or the V.C. The chopper must have recognized our frantic waving because they turned the light off quickly. Once the light was off, we dove for cover in a drainage ditch. The ditch must have been filled with muck and sewage from the time Buddha was a baby, because it was deep and rank. The chopper flew off, and we left the safety of the ditch behind, but not the smell. I'm afraid that would be with us for some time to come.

For the third time that night, we tried to enter Bamboo Alley. We were all in line, spread apart from each other by a space of three feet and moving slowly. Why it chose this time to spook I'll never know, but a cow crashed to its feet, for the last time in its life. As one, we turned and fired at the "enemy". When we had regrouped again at the street, we all knew something had died that night, and we were all quite sure it wasn't the V.C. Knowing this, Gary radioed in that we had made contact with the enemy, had broken contact, and would wait in place for sunrise. Over and out.

As the sun was rising, we assured the farmer we would be back later in the morning to pay for the cow, and no, we didn't want what was left of the cow. Like I said, it was a bizarre night.

The last night patrol of March was also a memorable adventure.

The Captain, or CO of our company, flew up the last week of March from Cu Chi, to see how our platoon operated. He wanted to take part in everything we did as a unit. He spent time at each of our posts, constantly gathering information. To me, this was the way an officer should act, and we told him so. If his trip was to also evaluate Lieutenant Jones, he got an ear full. He experienced more in one week than Lieutenant Jones did in an entire year.

His week started out with Gary and me at Main Gate. It was early in the morning when he had his first chance to get hot, sweaty, and dirty. The Captain was wearing very neat, starched fatigues. He was not destined to stay that way. One of the first trucks to leave the base camp that day was a Vietnamese garbage truck. Normally, we took care of our own garbage, but they had been hired to empty the grease pits at all the mess halls.

As we joked about how they could separate the mess

hall food from the grease pits, Gary was breaking a branch off a nearby tree. He jumped up into the truck and took the tops off the fifty-five gallon drums. I noticed all the workers laughing and joking about Gary gagging, until they saw he was going to push his stick into the barrel. The laughing stopped abruptly. "Heads up, Captain. Something's not right," I said, as I fingered the safety on my M-16 to the off position. Gary's stick only went down half way into the barrel before striking something. "I hate to say this, but we have to reach into these barrels," Gary said. Since I was getting everyone out of the truck and covering them, the Captain jumped up into the truck to help. I was out of sight of the Captain and Gary, but I could hear them gagging and throwing up. Once the reinforcements for which I had radioed arrived, I jumped up into the truck.

I saw Gary and the Captain, stripped of their shirts, with grease, slime, and mold up to their necks and faces. Piled next to the barrels were about twenty short wave radios in plastic bags. They must have been stolen from the P.X.

What I felt was admiration for the Captain. Not only did he dig in to help, but he also stayed with us until we were relieved of our duty for the day. He wore his slime like a medal.

For anyone with whom they came in contact, relief of duty couldn't come soon enough. Just before we were to be relieved, we had an accident that clogged the Main Gate area.

A three quarter ton pick-up truck approached us with the bridge guard relief. As we were talking to him, a tank retriever came rumbling down the road. A tank retriever, which is twice the size of a tank, retrieves tanks that are broken down. The tracked vehicle was moving at a high rate of speed toward us. When the driver applied the brakes to slow down, his hatch cover slammed down on his head, knocking him unconscious.

Before another crew member could completely stop the vehicle, it slowly crept up and over the pick-up. Since it was moving slowly, the driver and the guards jumped, squirmed, and pushed their way out of the truck. By the time the tank retriever was stopped, the entire pick-up stood about a foot and a half tall. It was crushed, but everyone, including the driver, was unhurt. There were a few scratches, bumps, and bruises, but it could have been a disaster.

As we pulled away from Main Gate, the Captain commented about what a day it had been. "Most people think we're just at war over here, but we have a lot of everyday problems to deal with as well. The war just adds more stress to an already stressful life."

"You'll find out just how stressful when you go on Night Patrol," I said. I had no idea how well he would learn that lesson when I said it, but he would learn a lesson about stress and leadership.

The last thing our Captain would experience for the week was Night Patrol. As my squad gathered to discuss the fine details of that night's patrol, Captain VanKampen made it clear he would be along, but only as an observer. "Lieutenant Jones will be in charge," he said. We all burst out laughing because we thought he was joking. When he asked what was so funny, we said, "The Lieutenant has never been on patrol, and he has only been off the base camp on one or two occasions."

With a face flushed with anger, he left the hootch headed for the Lieutenant's quarters. Ten minutes later he was back. "We'll both be going along as observers. Sorry for the interruption. Please continue," he said.

Since we would have two newbies along, we decided an ambush in place would be best. We would move out from the

Vietnamese fort and move directly to the pottery factory. We would set our ambush on the raised, walled hill overlooking the field into which Bamboo Alley opened. The factory would be at our backs, and we would look out over a football size field. Our field of fire was approximately thirty feet below us. Twenty feet of brick wall and ten feet of natural open rise or hill were where we would be spread out. It was a perfect spot for an ambush, perfect for us.

The Captain and Lieutenant would be in the middle of the squad as we walked to our ambush site. Lux and Gary went over the finer points with the Captain and Lieutenant while the rest of us caught some shut eye.

Later that night I introduced Captain Van Kampen to our Vietnamese interpreter. "Nguyen will do all the talking, when, and if, we have to talk. Hopefully, we will return without a word being spoken," I said.

We spent the first hour of patrol in a downpour. Once everyone got wet and realized they would stay wet and miserable for the rest of the night, we used the rain to muffle our movement. We took a very direct, and speedy route to the pottery factory. I was on point, so, as we approached the area where we would set up for the night, I stopped the squad. Then I went ahead to scout our ambush position.

Since there were no doors in the doorways nor glass in the windows of the factory, I cut through the building. It was a two story building that was about forty feet wide and seventy-five feet long. I checked the upstairs first, and then looked out a window where we would spend the rest of the night. I had been in this factory many times and felt comfortable moving around it in the dark. I had to be careful I did not step on broken bits of pottery laying on the floor, or topple over piled up pots, but that wasn't too difficult. I moved silently back to where the squad waited and signaled them that it was safe. As they passed me, I counted them to make sure we didn't acquire any new unwanted members. The only unwanted member was Lieutenant Jones, but he wasn't new. As we sprawled out on top of the wall, the rain stopped, and the moon came out very brightly. We were laying elbow to elbow, fourteen on the wall, and two in the factory covering our backs. Since we had such a clear field of view in front of us and the factory at our backs, we felt we could whisper on occasion. The Lieutenant was laying at one end of the squad, next to Nguyen. The Captain was situated in the middle of the squad.

The first nuisance of the night was the mosquitoes. The air was thick with them, and it wasn't long before everyone was pulling out their small plastic bottles of bug dope. Everyone offered to share with the Captain. The Lieutenant would be one large lump by morning.

The next nuisance to come along were the rats. Rats constantly crawled across every part of your body. I hate rats. As quietly as possible, I tried to scare them off as did everyone. My attention was focused on a rat when I sensed everyone had stopped moving. Everyone's attention was focused on a flickering light coming down Bamboo Alley towards us. You could have cut the tension with a knife. The entire population of this country knew that you do not move around at night, no matter what. The flickering light moved out of Bamboo Alley and showed us a small boy and an adult male in the candle light. They proceeded across the field in our direction. Not a person moved, for we all knew there was more to this than met the eye. The man and boy were directly below us when I heard movement and whispering from the other side of the squad.

Suddenly, out of the stillness of the night, "Halt, who goes there?"

Halt, who goes there? I was dumbfounded. What idiot would blow our ambush? It was then that I put the voice of Lieutenant Jones and the idiotic statement together. There was more talk, and then Nguyen started talking in Vietnamese. I leaned over the edge to get a better view of the two below us. What I saw made me flush with anger. The "father" had raised his candle as if to better see us, but the motion of the candle caught my attention. He was signaling someone on the other side of the field. Slowly, he moved the candle back and forth while he carried on a conversation with Nguyen. One of the words I picked up on was Bac si. With that one word I knew his excuse was that he was taking his "son" to the doctor.

As senior member of this squad, and with nineteen days left in-country, I felt I had to speak for the squad. I crawled over close to the Lieutenant who was standing, fully illuminated by the candle. Staying out of the light, just in case someone fired at the Lieutenant, I said, in a barely contained whisper, "Do you realize what you've done? Every Viet Cong in the country now knows exactly where we are."

"I tell him no, but he no listen," said Nguyen.

"You just fell for a trick. The V.C. wanted to know where we were and you just told them, loud and clear. 'Halt, who goes there?' Where do you think you are? This isn't a game. The only reason you aren't dead right now is because, if they fired, all hell would rain down on them. But, I would dare bet there is an AK-47 aimed at your chest right now, " I said.

This last statement must have sunk in because he suddenly dropped to his knees.

"Nguyen, tell him we wouldn't shoot someone going to

the doctor, and Nguyen, tell him in those exact words," I said. "And finally, send him on his way with hopes his kid will feel better."

Exactly nine days later, in a different part of the village, the V.C. would try this same stunt again, only then we wouldn't have that dumb ass Lieutenant along. This time, the "father and son" would signal an all clear and five heavily armed Viet Cong would join them. They would all die in a hail of gunfire. But that's another story; this night wasn't over.

After the two Vietnamese left, I crawled back to Gary and Lux to discuss our options. "I'm not worried about a frontal attack, but if they set up a mortar, we're trapped. If we don't move fast, they could set up an ambush in several places on routes back to the fort," I said. A sudden cloud burst made our decision for us. "We'll use the rain to get us as far and as quietly away from here as we can. When it stops, we stop for the night. If it continues, we beat it back to the fort." Lux let the base camp know that we were returning to the ARVN fort so they could inform the Vietnamese that we were coming in. I said, "Thank God for the monsoon season." "Let's haul ass," said Gary.

From decision to movement only took seconds. We all, excluding the Lieutenant, knew the severity of our situation. The Captain understood the value of experience and allowed us free rein when it came time to give orders. He had the common sense to step back and listen. He even went so far as to tell the Lieutenant he wanted the Lieutenant in front of him where he could keep an eye on him. This would prove to be a mistake.

We took a round-about route back to the fort because we thought the V.C. would think we would take the most direct route. Once again, cat and mouse. We started out as the cat tonight, but soon became the mouse. There was no shame involved; we would live to become the cat another night.

The rain didn't let up; in fact, it increased as we made our way back to the fort. I breathed a sigh of relief as I passed through the gate. One more time I started counting my men...thirteen, fourteen. Oh, my God, I was missing two! I rushed back into the street to see if I could see two more guys pulling up the rear, but I couldn't see very far into the rain.

As I gathered the squad together inside, I already knew who was missing. If it had just been the Lieutenant, I would have left him out there, but I couldn't do that to the Captain.

Everyone volunteered to go back out, but I thought we could do this quicker if we kept the numbers down. Lux, Gary, and I were soon back out on the street. The rain had once again stopped, but everything was still dripping. The moon would break through the clouds occasionally, but for the most part, it remained very dark. We didn't want haste to get us killed, but we also felt the need to hurry. We retraced our path, leap frogging each other doorstep to doorstep. As we approached a wide open crossing, we gathered together.

"We're half way through town at this point," I had said before being interrupted. "I just saw a flash of light on the other side of the street about two stores down," said Gary.

"What kind of light?" I asked, just as the aroma of cherry tobacco drifted our way. "Oh my God, the Lieutenant just lit up his pipe. Can you believe it? Should we shoot him?" I said half in jest.

"Yes," they said, without the slightest hint of jest.

"When we approach them, we'll have to be careful they don't shoot us. We'll speak to them when we get close," I said.

We approached to within ten feet, and they still hadn't seen or heard us. The Lieutenant had put his pipe out, but you could tell exactly where they were from the tobacco smell. They were huddled under the front stoop of a store.

"Captain, don't shoot. It's Lux, Minnick, and Coney," I said. I thought if he heard our names he would know it wasn't a trick. As we came in closer I said, "Don't talk now. I'll take point, Lux will get in between you two, and Gary will pull up the rear. Let's hat up."

We made it back to the fort without incident, but once inside, we had one hot Captain to deal with.

The Lieutenant was told to wait inside while the Captain talked to the three of us. We weren't sure what to expect.

"I have never seen such ineptitude in my entire military career, or in my life, as far as that goes," the Captain began. He was livid. We had a good idea who he was talking about, at least we hoped we knew, so we just let him rant and rave. As if we could have stopped him or even interrupted him. He was on a roll.

The gist of his tirade, as we explained it to the rest of the squad, was this: In the heavy rain, he'd followed Jones, and Jones had allowed too much of a separation between himself and the guy in front of him. Everyone behind them recognized where they were by familiar landmarks. Because the Lieutenant had never left the base camp, he had no idea where he was once they'd separated from us. When they figured out they were on their own and lost, they decided to get out of the rain and wait for our return. They had hidden under the porch, and the Captain told Jones to watch one way and he would watch the other. It about blew his mind when the Lieutenant lit his pipe. He said he was almost speechless, but he did manage to let him know that that pipe had better be put out immediately.

As stupid as it was, I'm not sure we would have found them if Gary hadn't spotted the strike of the Lieutenant's match. They had wandered just far enough off our route.

Before Captain Van Kampen left for Cu Chi, he spent several hours with Lieutenant Jones in private. No one knows what was said, but the Lieutenant did seem to try to do a better job afterwards. He just wasn't officer material.

March ended by going out like a lamb. With the coming of April, I had fourteen days left in-country. They would prove to be an exciting fourteen days.

April, 1968

When I arrived in-country, I often wondered if I would make it to another April. There were many times throughout the year that the thought had come up, but here it was. Just fourteen days; I was truly short. With the coming of April, I made myself a promise. It was that I would be exceptionally careful for the next two weeks. After what I had been through, I could do two weeks standing on my head.

It wasn't a written rule, but it was custom to keep the short timers on the base camp when their days got down into the teens. Since I had fourteen days left, I was determined to stay on the base camp. At least, that was my intention.

Day One: Late in the afternoon on April one, Papa-San ordered me to pick up two new replacements at the airport. I grabbed my M-16, steel pot, and flak jacket, jumped in the jeep and was off. A C-41 cargo plane came in right on time. After disembarking, I told my two newbies to hurry up. I explained to them that it wasn't safe to be this close to such a large target. I thought I should start educating them right away. They probably thought I was trying to scare them, but they didn't argue. As we started to pull out, I heard Papa-San's familiar voice come over the radio. He didn't use a call sign because I wasn't on patrol. "Mike, this is Ferret Two. We just got a call that three P.O.W.'s have to be picked up from the field. Do you have your weapon, flak jacket, and steel pot?" he asked. Looking at the two newbies who had none of those things, I responded, "Yes." If they had had a weapon, they would have been on their first flight out to the boondocks. Papa-San came back on, "Everyone else is assigned or sleeping. Meet the chopper that's warming up. Good luck, out." He had just said "Out" when it hit me. I responded back, "Ferret Two, this is Mike, April fool. Ha, ha. You almost had me, over." Papa-San came back, "No joke. Look at the choppers. There's only one, and it's waiting for you, short timer. Ferret Two, out."

As the chopper lifted off, I watched the two newbies drive away in my jeep.

I had no way to communicate with the pilots, so I had no way to know where we were going, not that it mattered. I just wanted to have a general idea where home was in case we went down.

I caught the attention of one of the door gunners and held out my hands in a questioning manner. He answered by pointing toward Cambodia. I suddenly felt the need to zip my flak jacket up. He also touched one hand to the other, quickly pulling it off, and shook it. Damn, the landing would be hot. Next, he pointed to my steel pot and my butt. The message was, when we get close, sit on your helmet. The helmet would slow down any bullets that might come up through the bottom of the chopper. Very funny! I smiled back at him.

If he was trying to scare me, it was working. But I really believed he was trying to help me. It was turning into one of those beautiful sunsets as we approached a ring of tanks in a small clearing. Ten or twelve tanks in a circle, firing at what seemed to me, unseen targets that were way too close.

We circled overhead at a very high altitude, waiting for someone on the ground to tell us to come in. When the word came we dropped like a rock, right into the center of the ring. I saw a G.I., struggling with three tied and blindfolded prisoners, approaching us. I jumped out of the chopper, ran about thirty yards, and grabbed the first prisoner's arm. Crouching over I pulled, pushed, and dragged him toward the chopper.

The pilot made a fist and pumped it up and down, signaling me to pick up the speed. When I got to the chopper, the door gunner helped me lift them onto the floor of the chopper. One of the prisoners seemed almost plump in comparison to the other two. He had to be a high ranking officer, even though he was dressed like the other two.

We got them situated on the floor and were lifting off before I could sit down. As we passed just beyond the ring of tanks, we started drawing fire from the enemy. Green tracers filled the air. The tanks did as much as they could for us, and our door gunners were spraying the jungle as we continued to rise. I pumped several magazines of ammo at some of the spots the green tracers were coming from. I could see the path of tracers leading right into the side and belly of the chopper.

We took quite a few hits, but we climbed into the growing night sky and safety.

Within the hour we were touching down on the helipad in Dau Tieng. As I started to escort my P.O.W.'s, I looked over my shoulder and counted at least a dozen bullet holes in the chopper. Lord, stick with me for thirteen more days!

Day Two: Since April Fool's Day will live in my memory forever, I thought day two of April could only be better.

I tried sleeping in the bunker. I strung my hammock, but couldn't sleep. It was too uncomfortable, and the mosquitoes were having a feast. Half way through the night, I crawled into my cot and the safety of my mosquito net.

I was feeling pretty groggy from lack of sleep when I started patrolling the base camp with Gary. I had decided we would try to stick to the perimeter of the base camp, because the mortars fell most often toward the center of the camp. We were headed north on the east side of the camp, when I noticed yellow and green paper all over the ground ahead of us. As we got closer, we could see that it was a flock of parakeets feeding in the road. I got as close as I could and turned the jeep off to enjoy the sight. There had to be fifty or more identical birds picking at gravel or bugs.

It seemed so peaceful and quiet. The way life should be. We had stopped in a part of the base camp where they stored the highly flammable chopper fuel. It was stored in huge bladders. The bladders were supposed to give enough so that incoming shells would not detonate, thus avoiding an explosion and fire. No one was allowed to live close to them, so I'm not sure the theory worked.

With our engine off and no one near by, it seemed extraordinarily quiet. It was so quiet there was no mistaking the distinctive sound of a mortar passing over our heads. By the time the shell exploded, Gary and I were out of the jeep and pressing ourselves into the mound of dirt surrounding the gas bladders. Two more shells fell in quick succession nearby before Gary and I opened our eyes and stared at each other. It had dawned on us both, that the only thing separating us from thousands of gallons of highly explosive gas was a small mound of dirt.

Without a word to each other, we made a run for the jeep. I started the jeep and shot past the spot where the parakeets were, heading for the safety of a bunker further down the perimeter line.

From the safety of the closest bunker, I thought about those parakeets sitting at the top of some tree, free from all this human madness.

Just twelve more days, and I'd be on my own freedom bird, leaving all this madness behind.

Day Three: Day three was just like day two, only this time I was on the west side of the camp with Lux. I wanted to be as far way from the gas storage area as I could get, but I was running out of camp. About twenty rounds fell, during mid-afternoon, while I watched from the safety of a perimeter bunker. My plan worked to perfection.

We had just gotten to the top of a small hill along the bunker line, when the first round hit the center of the camp. We pulled our jeep over next to a bunker and crowded around the door with five guards from the bunker. From our vantage point, we could watch G.I.s scamper for cover as the rounds fell. It looked like someone had just kicked an ant hill.

Being the short timer in the group, and not entirely stupid, I stood in the doorway leaning my shoulder against the door frame with my feet crossed. The rounds were being walked up the center of the camp, when for some odd reason, a stray round landed thirty yards in front of us. Regrettably, I untangled my feet too slowly for the six people that suddenly wanted to be inside. They bowled me over and proceeded to step on me as they scrambled for the farthest reaches of the bunker. I picked my aching body up, dusted myself off, and shut all the laughter off with one comment, "Eleven days, boys, eleven days."

Day Four: Day four in my countdown found me once again hugging the perimeter of the base camp. Papa-San's familiar voice came across the radio with a request for me to pick up another replacement at the airport. Letting him know I didn't like the assignment, I responded, "Ferret Two, would that be the airport located in the center of the base camp?" When he came back, I could hear him laughing. "That would be the one, and be advised, the only one. In and out. No sweat, short timer. Ferret Two, out."

No sweat, right. I considered the airport as I would the red bullseye on a target. I decided I'd wait at the end of the runway, on the perimeter, until the plane landed. I would continue to wait until the newbie had time to get off the plane before I drove down the runway to pick him up.

The lumbering C-41 dropped out of the sky at a steep angle to avoid sniper fire from the rubber trees, touched down and rolled to a stop. I started the jeep and watched the flurry of activity as they tried to unload the aircraft as fast as possible. After three or four minutes, I started down the runway at a high rate of speed.

A hi-lo was moving up to the back of the aircraft, as people were filing out. The engines of the plane and the hi-lo were very noisy as I approached the plane.

I never heard or saw the first round hit. What caught my attention was a fifty-five gallon oil drum shoot a hundred yards straight up into the air. I don't know what was in the barrel, but its exit from the base camp was quite impressive.

Choppers coming in were rerouted to act as a reactionary force, so only two rounds fell. One round hit the barrel, the other round landed near the plane. The only part of the plane damaged was the side window, next to the pilot. Unfortunately for the pilot, he was sitting there. One piece of shrapnel entered his left cheek and exited through his right cheek, taking most of his teeth with it.

The newbie and I loaded him into my jeep and raced for the med-evac hospital.

As I sloshed down my jeep with a pail of water to rid it of blood, I said to the newbie, "Welcome to Vietnam." You would have thought that would have been enough for day four, but it was a long way from being done.

Since the only radio station we could get was the Armed Forces radio station, everyone on the base camp heard the broadcast describing the murder of Martin Luther King at the same time.

I heard it just before I was going to eat supper. As the newbie and I were walking to the mess hall, I mentioned it to him. His comment was, "Who's he?" About all I could tell him was that he was a minister that had an interest in civil rights. In other words, I didn't know much about him either.

Before the end of the night, we both would learn what a significant and sad event this was. Coming from a small community in Michigan, I can honestly say, I didn't realize that everyone didn't have the same freedoms and rights as I did.

It had just gotten dark, and we were waiting for our nightly dose of mosquito dope from Korean Carl when Papa-San approached us. "We've got a situation at graves registration," he said. "Apparently someone got fragged." Fragging is a term used when a fragmentation grenade is used to settle a dispute or to remove an inept leader. It didn't happen very often, but it did happen. Most of the time, just the mention of a fragging would settle a dispute, or make an officer think about his men rather than his career. Anyway you look at it, or try to justify it, it was still murder.

In a very short amount of time, the entire platoon was on its way to the graves registration company area. Graves registration is where the bodies of American soldiers were prepared for transportation back to the states.

We could tell immediately that something was wrong, because the entire company area was bathed in light. In an entire year, I had never seen the lights on after dark. This had to be serious.

A captain came up to us and told us that a hand grenade had been thrown into a hootch occupied by two sergeants. One was dead, the other was in serious condition. "Why all the lights?" I asked. "We're giving Charlie a perfect target."

He said, "Another hand grenade was thrown and shots fired when we tried to investigate what happened. We need you to secure the area."

Gary asked why this had happened, and the answer he got made me sick. Apparently, the two sergeants had made some comments about the death of Martin Luther King. Something to the effect that it was about time somebody got him. That comment, plus the fact that they were plain and simply ignorant, almost caused a riot in their mess hall. In any case, they made some enemies in the last place in the world that you need more enemies.

That was the situation we were forced to deal with. We had to get those lights out, but to do that would place us in a very vulnerable position.

Gary and I thought we should try to settle down the large group of black soldiers who had gathered and wouldn't disperse for the captain.

How do you tell a large, angry crowd that you understand their anger, and that we were not the enemy. In fact, this whole situation made me sick.

I had spent an entire year under very stressful conditions, and nothing like this had ever happened. All the different races got along with each other. Sure, there were people you didn't like, but that was based on personality, not race. We shared everything with each other: food, water, clothes, stories, and problems. I had been told many personal things about their families, sometimes more than I cared to know, but that was the way we were. We were tight. We cared about each other. That was why this tore at me. This incident was tearing apart a world with which I had become very comfortable.

Gary and I walked up to a group of soldiers, with whom we were somewhat familiar, and plead our case. "This isn't what Dr. King would have done, or wanted done in his name. Help us settle things down, and let's get these lights out." After a few minutes of listening to complaints, I thought the situation seemed less tense. Some of the black soldiers in our platoon were saying that this struggle needed to be carried out back in the states, not here where we could be killed at any second.

There were no further comments because a grenade exploded in a hootch in back of us. We asked the soldiers to help us calm others, and they responded by filling in our ranks as we moved forward. Because of everyone's cooperation, we were able to diffuse a very volatile situation.

The grenade had been thrown into the same hootch the sergeants had been in. One of our guys had been standing at the door, and had heard the klunk as the grenade hit and rolled across the floor. He dove away from it, but still suffered minor wounds.

No one was caught for either fragging. We eventually restored the peace and turned out the lights. Strangely, the V.C. left us alone. They must have been as confused as we were by the night's events.

We escaped the night with only one of our platoon hurt, but in a sense we were all wounded. Deep in our hearts, I think we all knew things would be different from now on. This was a wound begun in the United States and left to fester in Vietnam. This country had enough of its own sores; it didn't need any more imported by us. This night would be a sad scar on a year of friendships that went way beyond the insignificance of race or color.

Day four finally ended in the early hours of day five, but the problems that were created that night would continue for years.

Day Five: Day five was a piece of cake; I had Main Gate guard duty. The only excitement all day was when Bic caught a scorpion.

It was the biggest, blackest scorpion I had seen all year. It had decided to cross the street in broad daylight. Big mistake. I drew my pistol and was about to eliminate the enemy scorpion when Bic yelled, "No shoot, no shoot." She ran over and lightly stepped on the scorpion. She was wearing only the shower shoes she usually wore.

As she gently held it down, she undid the string that held her conical hat on her head. She then made a loop on one end of the string. She moved her foot so just the stinging point could be seen, and slipped the loop over it. She then suspended the scorpion away from her body saying, "Much medicine." I have no idea what kind of medicine was made from a scorpion, but she took it home and kept it in a cage.

Other than that incident, it was a very quiet day, just the way I liked it. That evening, I sat down to write Laurie my last letter from Vietnam. I got my lawn chair situated close to my fan, popped a Lone Star Beer, flipped the radio on, and counted my blessings.

The announcer, some Saigon cowboy trying to sound important, came on the radio with some late breaking news broadcast.

Because of the escalating problems brought about by the seizing of the U.S.S. Pueblo by the North Koreans on January 25, President Johnson will divert troops on their way to Vietnam to South Korea. President Johnson may extend rotation dates on returning soldiers from Vietnam and Korea, or even cancel them. On-going negotiations with the North Koreans will determine future actions."

There was more, but the only part I heard was that I might be extended. Normally G.I.s can find humor in any situation, and teasing will go on under the most difficult of times, but this was no laughing matter. No one said anything, We were all affected by the taking of the Pueblo.

Gary asked, "What are we going to do?"

"It don't mean nothing. Nothing means nothing," I replied and tried to believe it.

Now came the hard part. Dear Laurie,...

Day Six: Because of commitments to other units, we were short handed, which meant that today, and for the next few days I would have to take Checkpoint Three and Four.

Since the taking of the Pueblo, I had a changed attitude. I still considered myself short, but didn't know how short. Life had to go on, I hoped.

Sniping at the checkpoints was almost a daily thing, but not extremely dangerous. Charlie had to shoot from such a distance, and at such an angle, that he was rarely even close to hitting anyone. We had cut trees back, taking away cover which proved effective. The shooting was more unnerving than anything else.

A nightly reactionary force came out to the checkpoint to escort everyone back to the base camp. It was made up of the same group that escorted us out in the morning. As the sun went down, at least twenty-five of us made the mad rush back to the base camp. Every day, at a different time, and in a different way so as not to get caught in a routine the V.C. could pick up on, we provided protection for the checkpoint guards. It was a very effective way to provide some safety. One night as we were preparing to leave, a small force of V.C. attacked us. Papa-San called for a second reactionary force, and we counter-attacked them. A small ARVN unit had moved in behind the V.C., and we were to act as the hammer in a hammer and anvil ambush. The V.C. were shocked. We didn't usually attack, and they started to retreat into the trap. They left a machine gun team to cover their retreat. We let the machine gun keep us pinned down, because we didn't want to get caught in the cross fire of the trap. It wasn't causing any damage anyway. As it got darker, one of the other squad members passed me saying, "I'm too short for this, I've only got fifty-seven days left." At that, he set off at a run for the base camp. Papa-San yelled, "Get back here." He didn't even slow down. "Shoot him," he said. I was the closest person to Papa-San and heard him clearly. I placed my sight on his back and knew I could hit him square. "I can't do it, Papa-San," I said. I was angry enough but couldn't do it. He had committed the cardinal sin for a G.I.

You do not leave your buddies on the field of battle, alive, wounded, or dead. Above and beyond that, I was shorter than he was by almost fifty days.

We heard the ARVN's gunfire springing their ambush and assumed they were successful. Their gunfire signaled us it was time for our retreat.

Papa-San had a long night ahead of him. He could not allow anyone to get away with desertion. As for me, I was a day shorter.

Day Seven: After Checkpoint Three, Checkpoint Four was a piece of cake. Only three people passed through the checkpoint all day. Two newbies, Carter and Johnson, and I had just opened our C-ration cans for lunch when a little boy approached us. I would guess he was eight or nine years old. He stood about five feet from us with his hands behind his back, which wasn't an uncommon stance for little kids. Around Dau Tieng they didn't hold out their hands to beg food like they did near Saigon. They just stood patiently, staring with those big brown eyes. C-rations are placed upside down so you can't read the labels and grab the best meals. When I got my C-rations, I saw I was stuck with ham and lima beans. I have yet to meet anyone that likes that meal, so I gave it to the kid. When he brought his hands out in front of him to accept the can, he was holding an M-79 round from a grenade launcher. We all froze. He could kill us all very easily.

He had brought the dud to us for a reward. Not knowing how to go about it, and not being able to speak English, he waited patiently for us to discover it. In pantomime we showed him how to set it down, and then we all backed away. The little boy was reluctant to leave his treasure where anyone could grab it, but we gave him quite a few piasters to leave it.

We radioed for bomb disposal and Bic to come out to Checkpoint Four. Through Bic, we tried to tell the little boy the danger he was in. "When you find duds, do not bring them to us. We will go to it," I said.

The little boy said others may find it and collect the reward while he is gone looking for Americans, or the Americans will think he is leading them into a trap. He had a point. I wish I could have given him twenty dollars to not pick up duds, but I'd be swamped by every kid in Vietnam. I knew I couldn't convince him not to bring in duds, so I drew a line in the dirt and told him not to come any closer than the line if he had a dud. Bic explained it all to him, and off he went with his reward and his ham and lima beans.

In every way, every day was an adventure in Vietnam, and my adventure was one day closer to ending.

Day Eight: Day eight was a day of celebration. A new commander took over the Vietnamese fort. We decided to have a dinner and an exhibition soccer and football game in his honor.

We played the games in the morning when it was as cool as it would be all day.

The soccer game was a disaster. A local Vietnamese team ran around us like we were standing still, and many times we were. Not many of us understood the game. The part we understood was the score, ten to zero.

After the soccer game, we put on an exhibition football game. My platoon played against an engineer platoon. The only equipment we had was the football. Needless to say, it got pretty rough. The Vietnamese crowd loved it. I'm sure they didn't have the faintest idea what was going on, but they cheered anytime someone was knocked down or tackled. I don't believe one player walked away without an injury. Nothing serious, just cuts, bruises, bumps, sprains, and strains. What a blast.

I played high school football and I loved it, but this game was just as memorable. It was one of the better times I had in Vietnam. What set this game apart from the high school games were the machine guns on all corners of the field and the small band playing their hearts out, with M-16s strapped to their backs.

The day ended with me one day shorter and every muscle in my body aching. It was great.

Day Nine: Pete and I were called on to escort the Checkpoint Three guards into position. Our part was to pull down the road where we had almost hit a mine, and cover the rubber trees while everyone else settled in at the checkpoint. Everything went off without a hitch. The all clear, thank-you, and see you later came across the radio, signaling us that our part was finished until sun down. Pete looked at me and said, "Let's go down to the school and leave a message." The school was actually three deserted Michelin buildings that the V.C. used to train new recruits. The walls were covered with drawings and writings. In charcoal they diagramed how to strip down and clean various weapons. I had only been there twice. It was just a little too far away from reinforcements. It was less than a half mile east of the base camp and less than a quarter mile north of the checkpoint, but that was too far. It was Indian country.

I looked at him and said, "Pete, how short am I?"

"That's all the more reason to do it. One last parting shot at the V.C.," he said.

"Parting shot? That's exactly what I'm afraid of. Just who will get that parting shot in first?" I asked.

"Let's make it quick," I said, as I zipped my flak jacket shut.   In less than a minute, we were there. I picked up a piece of charcoal from an old campfire and wrote 'Sat Cong' in large letters on the outside wall.   The Vietnamese death wish, I thought, was appropriate as my parting shot.

Pete did the same on the next building, while I covered him. When he was finished, we sprinted back to the jeep and off we went at a high rate of speed. We hadn't gone fifty yards when a shot rang out from the woods. We both responded by ducking down, and the problem with that was that Pete was driving. He started to fish tail, and I knew he was going to lose it. Somehow the jeep turned completely around on this narrow road and continued down the road backwards. For a fleeting moment I thought we were going to make it. No such luck. The jeep turned on its side and slid into the concertina wire. This fence of concertina wire was three rolls of barb wire piled on top of each other.

Somehow, my seat came right out of the jeep and I rode it straight into the barbed wire. I went in backwards so that the seat and my flak jacket took most of the punishment the barbed wire had to give. My arms and legs were ripped up, but I was more concerned about being entangled in the barb wire. My biggest fear was that the sniper would walk up and shoot me as I struggled to free myself. I resolved myself to the fact I was going to have to hurt myself more to avoid being shot.

I began ripping my arms and legs loose from the barb wire. The whole time I was whispering, "Pete, are you all right?" His reply was "Man, I'm sorry. I'm all right, are you?" He was on the other side of the jeep out of my sight. "A few cuts and bruises, but I'll be all right. Why didn't he pump a few more rounds at us?" I asked.

"He must have been in a tree, and we rolled just far enough to be out of his line of sight. Let's get out of here," he said. After I was free, we rocked the jeep back onto its wheels, retrieved my seat and rifle, and were on our way.

A stop at the medics for antibiotics and bandaging and day nine, thank God, was history.

Day Ten: Late in the afternoon on day ten, Papa-San called Lux and me into headquarters. We were patrolling the post when he radioed that he wanted to talk to us in person. My first thought was, great, here we go again. He's going to talk about something he can't put out over the air. This is not good.

Papa-San started off by saying "Don't get excited. This assignment will be a piece of cake. All you have to do is meet a convoy of trucks and tanks at the bridge around 1600 hours. When you make contact with the convoy, escort them to the Main Gate. Stay at Main Gate to count the vehicles that pass to make sure there are no stragglers. Pete and Gary will pick them up at Main Gate and take them to the area where they will spend the night. They will move out again in the morning, but that's not our problem. Any questions?"

"Piece of cake," we answered.

It all appeared to be like he had said, a piece of cake. We sat down by the bridge, where we could see for miles. We linked up with the convoy. We escorted them to Main Gate. We headed for our hootch. Day ten was over and done. "No question, no problem," I said.

Lux and I had been sitting at the bridge from 1500 hours, or as we close-to- being-civilians like to say, 3 p.m. It was now 5 p.m. I was starting to get this sinking feeling that we might be out after dark when Lux said, "I see a cloud of dust. It's got to be them."

Lux cranked the engine over, and I radioed Gary that we were on the move. We shot out over the bridge as fast as that jeep would go and went a mile past it. We turned around before the tree line and watched the lead tank barrel down on us. We assumed at least 150 more vehicles were behind him, but because of the dust we couldn't see them. Lux leaped our jeep out in front, and I signaled the tank commander by hand to follow us. He gave us a thumbs up, and we were off. When we came in sight of the base camp and Pete and Gary, I radioed them, "They're all yours." I then signaled the tank commander to follow Gary as we pulled off to the side. This was all accomplished without losing a single mile per hour. They were moving past us at a high rate of speed and covering us with their dust. I tied a handkerchief around my face so I could breath, and Lux did the same. Twenty-five tanks, fifty trucks, and five tankers had passed us when I saw the window of an approaching truck disintegrate. I knew instantly it had been shot out. I tried to get Lux's attention, but with all the noise and dust it was impossible. More shots were fired. You couldn't hear them, but you could see the damage the bullets were causing. Lux finally saw one hit, and he looked at me. Since he was on the other side of the street, I signaled for him to come to my side. I assumed his side of the street was from where the sniper was firing. Getting across the street wouldn't be easy; these trucks and tanks were moving fast. The trucks that had radios knew that they would be sniped at when they approached Main Gate, so their speed kept increasing as they got closer to us.

When Lux finally reached me, I yelled in his ear, "I don't think the sniper is interested in us, or he may not even see us in all this dust, but when that last truck goes by, we'll be the only targets left. Let's not stick around."

Several more trucks were hit, but no one was hurt seriously, and more importantly, no one stopped. After the last truck went by in a cloud of dust, we ran for our jeep. We had backed it into a huge bush to conceal it and help keep the dust off it.

We knew from experience that running a zig zag route back to the jeep, and bending over at the waist would offer a difficult target. Lux jumped in the driver's seat, and I'd almost made it to the passenger side when I was knocked down. I couldn't figure out what had happened. All I knew was that my face hurt, and I couldn't see out of my right eye.

I picked myself up off the ground, jumped in the jeep, and we sped off. "What happened?" we both said at the same time. "I don't know, but I'm afraid I lost my eye," I said. I was bent over with my hand cupped over my eye, and all I could see were stars flashing in my head. When we reached the safety of the base camp, I sat up and looked at my hand. It was full of blood, and I still couldn't see.

"What does it look like," I asked?

"You look like a giant, dust covered Bull Frog! Your eye is bulging out and bleeding. You also have a cut under your eye. Hang on, we'll have you at the med-evac in nothing flat," Lux said.

He wasn't kidding. We just about slid through the front door with the jeep.

"My buddy needs help," yelled Lux to a medic.

"There aren't any doctors on duty, but I'll look at him," the medic said. "Lay down, and let me have a look."

As he leaned over me, with my good eye and my nose, I could see and smell that he'd been drinking.

"You sure you know what you're doing?" I asked.

"No sweat," was his reply as he injected my face with a pain killer. As my entire head and neck went numb, I watched as his needle came closer to my eye. I was starting to see fuzzy images through my damaged eye, but I was so numb I couldn't even blink to clear the tears and blood away. I couldn't feel the needle or the stitches but every time he pulled one tight he would just about lift my head off the table. When he finished, he placed a patch over my eye and said to return in a week to remove the stitches and to check my vision.

Through numb lips I tried to say, "Going home, three days, short."

"Have your own doctor look at it when you get home then," the medic said.

I figured out I must have run into the jeep antenna. When we'd backed the jeep into the bush, the antenna had bent down and forward. What I knew for sure was that day ten ended back at the hootch, with my buddies teasing me and cold beer running down my numb face.

Day Eleven: I started day eleven paired with a newbie. My job would be to school him on the finer points of Vietnam and survival. I got his attention by saying, "What I'm going to show and tell you today may decide whether or not you make it out alive in 364 days." I just about choked on 364 days; it seemed like an eternity.

We started by touring the village. I tried to show him dangerous places, hiding places, and escape routes that he would have to memorize.

I tried to get him to understand the importance of always covering your back. In crowds, get a buddy to cover your back, or put your back against a wall. Don't trust anyone, and be suspicious of every situation you encounter. That was a most difficult lesson to learn, and one that had to be learned well---a lesson I learned so well it would effect the rest of my life.

We entered a side alley on the southwest side of the village, a seldom patrolled area. The V.C. had been in town the night before. It was evident because of the sheets of propaganda blowing around on the ground and tacked to trees. I told him to pick it up while I covered him. He picked up an armful and brought it back to the jeep. I set it all on fire while he returned for more. As I watched the fire and the surrounding area, I noticed he'd stepped out of sight, around the corner of a house. I hurriedly stomped out the fire and called to him. When I didn't get an answer, I ran to find him. As I rounded the corner of the house, my heart sunk. I saw him reaching up to pull a Viet Cong flag down. I screamed at him not to move, and he didn't! In a much calmer voice, I told him to back away from the flag the same way he had approached it. The V.C. know Americans love souvenirs, and they use that against us. My suspicions were correct. If he had pulled on the flag, he would have triggered a booby trap and would have, at the least, lost both feet. Because it was close to a house, we didn't set it off. We called for bomb disposal to disarm it.

As we pulled away from that alley, I knew a valuable lesson had been learned, but there were so many more to learn.

As we made our way back to the base camp, I wanted to show him the bridge and water tower and relay to him their importance to the base camp. As we approached the bridge, I told him to take in the whole scene.

"What do you see?" I asked.

"A river, a bridge, a couple of G.I.'s, and a truck," he said.

"Look at the little boy sitting on a coffee can. Doesn't it strike you odd that a ten year old would be sitting there all by himself? Where else in this country do you see anyone, especially a child, all by himself? As we approach him, watch what he does without staring."

Our route past him would take us within fifty feet of him. As I got parallel with him, I stopped the jeep. As soon as the jeep stopped, the little boy stood up, never looking at us and walked around the side of building. I knew he was gone, which was fine with me.

My newbie was understandably nervous about the coffee can, after his close call with the flag. I told him this wouldn't be an explosive because nobody could have been that cool while sitting on a bomb. When I tipped the can over with my foot, I found what I had expected to find. Neatly packaged in plastic bags was about two pounds of marijuana. I put it back in the can, picked it up, and headed for the jeep.

"What do we do with it?" the newbie asked.

"You obviously haven't looked at the "lawn" surrounding the M.P. headquarters. When they ask you to mow the grass that's exactly what you will be doing. We spread it out around the building, and it grows like crazy."

"That's unbelievable," he said.

I didn't say it, but I thought, you ain't seen nothing yet. You've got 364 unbelievable days ahead of you, if you make it. I always called him newbie; I didn't even want to know his name. Back in the states I might pick up a newspaper and see that he had been killed. I know that even though I had only spent a day with him, I would have felt I should have done more for him. I was already suffering from survivor's guilt, and I hadn't even left yet.

As we were spreading our grass seed outside of headquarters, Papa-San came out and said my orders were in. I would be departing early the next day, and I had the rest of the day off to clear up any loose ends.

This day for which I had long awaited (366 days to be exact), had finally arrived, and I didn't know quite how to respond. It seemed like my thoughts were colliding with each other inside my head. I couldn't complete any of them.

My emotions seemed as confusing as my thoughts. I felt happy for the most part. After all, I had been counting the days faithfully, everyday to this one, beginning with the day I landed in Vietnam. I was also, for some unexplainable reason, sad and scared. I was leaving this life, a dangerous life, but one I had become exceptionally good at. I had to face the uncertainty of the future.

Well, first things first. I had to pack and give away my possessions, and then I would have time to sort out my thoughts. Right now I felt like I was on a run away roller coaster; I had to put some order back into my life.

It didn't take long to pack up the few possessions I had, but it did take a long time to decide who would inherit the valuables I would leave behind. We always kidded each other about our personal stuff when we went out on an operation. We did this to ease the tension. We would say things like, "Can I have your fan if you're blown away, or can I have your boots?" In reality, nobody would have wanted the bad luck associated with a dead buddy's possessions. Although Bill used to ask if he could have my pictures of Laurie, and I think he meant it. I always told him, "No way G.I., I'm going to be buried with them."

My two most coveted possessions were my fan and my

lawn chair. Gary and Lux would get them, and I knew they would treasure them. Other items like my lucky jungle boots, hammock, knives, stationary, and camouflage clothing would be appreciated by the rest of the squad.

After the distribution of my vast wealth had been settled in my mind, I set out to find Bic. This part of leaving would be extremely hard, and I dreaded it. Time and again I had told her my parents would adopt her, if and when she wanted to leave Vietnam, but this was her country and these were her people. She was not ready to give up on either just yet.

When she saw me walking toward her, she must have read the look on my face because tears started to flow. "You go?" she asked.

"Yes, I leave tomorrow. As long as you work for the 25th Infantry Division, we can write, but you know the Americans won't stay forever. You have to plan for the future. If you change your mind about coming to the U.S., be sure to let me know. There is nothing more to say. Be careful, little sister." Before I turned to leave, I placed what Vietnamese piasters I had in her hand. I wouldn't need them and knew she would put the money to good use. She didn't ask for it, or expect it, or even count it. I knew she wouldn't; she liked me for who I was. I would miss her and worry about what might have happened to her for the rest of my life.

As I walked away, I asked God to watch over her. This country needed more people like her.

As the squad gathered for chow, I told them what I was leaving them. We also did the usual exchange of addresses and promises of getting together when we all returned to the world. As we were about to leave for the mess hall, Papa-San entered the hootch and said he needed the squad to reinforce the checkpoint which had just come under fire. Everyone grabbed their gear and were out the door, leaving me standing there in the middle of the hootch. I really felt my place was with my squad, but Papa-San wouldn't allow it.

I had lost my appetite, so I grabbed a beer out of our little refrigerator and walked outside to watch my last sunset in Vietnam. I leaned up against the bunker and stared at what promised to be a beautiful sunset.

I could hear shooting from the checkpoint and felt guilty for not being there with my friends. My being there probably wouldn't make a difference, but it might. What a strange land this was. I was caught between a blood red, peaceful, sunset and a bloody battle in which my squad was involved. Lord, what should I do? I received my answer immediately in the form of a bullet striking a rubber tree. It hit no more than a foot and a half to my left with a loud smack. One bullet, no more. It was probably intended for a bunker guard. It traveled across the helipad and delivered a message directly to me. That message: it's time to go home. My luck was used up. Suddenly, I felt at ease, like the decision had been made for me. A Viet Cong may have squeezed the trigger, but to me he was delivering a message from God. There must be something else I'm to do with my life. I moved to the other side of the bunker for protection, and continued to watch the sun set. No sense in pushing my luck.

Day Twelve: I was up and moving early on day twelve. All the good-bye's had been said, and more than a few beers had been drunk. I blamed my headache on my eye and stitches, but other than that, I felt good. The chopper would leave at 7:30 a.m., and nothing would keep me from being there. I was ready to leave for the chopper pad at 7:00 a.m. It was a two minute walk to my chopper. Papa-San yelled to me as I was on my way, "You're not through yet. Thought you'd get away easy, didn't you? You're already forgetting where you are. I've got a V.C. that has to be moved down to Cu Chi, and you're the only one going. Do you mind?" he said.

"Tie him up like a hog and blindfold him, and I'll take him. I'd only do this for you, Papa-San. Take care, and watch those boys for me." It wasn't much as good-bye's go, but, when we locked eyes for the last time, we knew there was no more that needed to be said.

As I waited for the prisoner to be delivered, I passed the time talking to the pilot. He said, "I've been shot at every day this week, in several places, all the way to Cu Chi, so we'll be flying low and fast. That way they can't get a bead on us."

He wasn't kidding. He was good, somewhat of a cowboy, but good. We didn't go over trees, we went right at them, and then slid right or left at the last second. His plan worked. As we flew over people, they hardly had time to look up, before we were over them and gone. He used the jungle for safety right down to where it turned into rice paddies. Then he dropped even lower. We ran parallel to a convoy, and I could look right into the driver's side window. We were low.

As we approached Cu Chi, he climbed steeply to a very high altitude. He looked at me and pointed ahead. I leaned forward and looked where the Cu Chi base camp should have been. In its place was a huge slow moving tornado of dust. They were having a dust storm, the likes of one I'd never seen before.

We circled the base camp, staying a long distance from the circling dust, waiting for it to subside. When it did, we dropped like a rock to the landing pad. I grabbed my bag and my prisoner and started for the P.O.W. camp. I had less than one hundred yards to walk to the prisoner-of-war gate. About fifty yards from the prison, the swirling dust storm began again. Within seconds, it was impossible to see. I forced my prisoner to lay on his stomach on the ground. I then pulled my poncho and poncho liner from my duffel bag. I covered him with my poncho and as I lay on my duffel bag, I covered myself with the liner. I put my foot on his back to feel if he moved because I couldn't see him in the dust. I also placed the barrel of my M-16 on the base of his neck. I was not going to let this guy get away and delay my exit from this country. We sat like that for at least fifteen minutes waiting for the wind to stop.

When it finally subsided, I shook a good four inches of dust off me. As I bent over to help the V.C. up, I found myself staring at a dust covered jeep not fifteen feet from us. The spot where I'd been forced to stop because of the dust storm was in the middle of the road. Fortunately, the jeep was also forced to stop because of the dust storm. The jeep turned out to be a military police jeep, and the two dust covered M.P.'s were friends of mine.

When we finished discussing the storm, and the close call we just had, they helped me deliver my prisoner to the P.O.W. camp. They then dropped me off at company headquarters.

The rest of the day was spent cleaning up my equipment before turning it in, and then cleaning myself up.

Day Thirteen: I was dropped off bright and early at the convoy marshaling area. I was wearing my summer dress khaki uniform. I had to wear jungle boots because my shoes had rotted away. Everyone knew I was going home. There were thumbs- up signs from everyone. They were happy for anyone that had made it. They all shouted out how short they were, which to me didn't seem short at all. With all the kidding and bantering back and forth, and happiness all about, I still had this nervous feeling. This was the first time in a year, except for my R & R in Hawaii, that I was without a weapon. In 365 days I'd never been further than an arm's length from a pistol and rifle. As I sat in the back of a truck with four other short timers, waiting for the convoy to start rolling, I became more and more anxious. I finally reached the point where I knew I had to take charge of my destiny. I couldn't and wouldn't allow myself to make this trip defenseless, not after what I had been through this past year. I had to at least have a chance to go down fighting. I'd come too far to have my life left to chance.

I jumped out of the truck and raced back to one of the machine gun jeeps. I explained my problem, and they were more than willing to give me a ride, and more importantly a weapon. I jacked a round into the M-16 and felt at ease with the world.

The trip to Long Binh was uneventful. It gave me time to soak in the surroundings one last time. The warm, moist air hitting me in the face from an open jeep and racing through an exotic and ancient land would never be experienced again. Thank goodness. Let me get on with my life.

Day Fourteen: Our freedom bird was scheduled to leave at 10:00 a.m. Of the two hundred G.I.'s leaving, no one was late. An officer from the military police said to all of us gathered on bleachers in a hanger, "If you have any explosives on your person, or in your baggage, we want you to dump it in these drums as you file out of the hanger to the jet. Remember: most of this stuff came down the Ho Chi Minh Trail and has never been subjected to the high altitudes your jet will reach. You don't want to take a chance with an accidental explosion now, do you?"

I had taken about twelve AK-47 bullets with me to give

to friends back home. They were in my pocket. I knew what he was saying couldn't really happen to bullets, but, as I went past the barrel, I dropped them in. Why take a chance?

We walked out onto the runway and waited in line for the newbies to disgorge from our freedom bird. As we were about to board, the M.P.'s raced up and ordered us to empty our duffel bags and strip down to our underwear (for those that had them). The M.P.'s walked up and down the line removing any contraband they found. The sergeant in front of me had a dismantled Thompson sub-machine gun taped to his legs, which he had to give up.

The pile continued to grow before my astounded eyes. And I'd worried about a few bullets. What a joke! Before me, in a pile, were weapons of every description: hand grenades, claymore mines, C-4 plastic explosives, and even a few artillery rounds.

As M.P.'s were loading the souvenirs into a truck, we were allowed to dress and board the jet. Not many people were talking; even as the jet taxied into position for take off, everyone was quiet. As the plane left the ground, the tension was broken. Everyone cheered, slapped each other on the back, and more than a few tears were shed.

As I placed the ear phones on my head to listen to some music, I realized I hadn't even looked out the window when we took off. It was time to look to the future. I closed my eyes, believing that I would now have a future. The first song played over the head set was the Temptations singing, "I've Passed This Way Before."

The End

Epilogue

After Vietnam, I returned to Holland, Michigan and married Laurie. We've raised three children. Jason, Ryan and Lyndsey will read many things in this book that will be new to them, and so will Laurie. Some of the stories I've used in the classroom over a twenty-seven year career in public education. Some of the stories I've never shared with anyone. Some stories will die with me, never to be shared with anyone.

Every soldier could write about their experiences in Vietnam, and I would encourage them to do it. Through gentle prodding by good friends, this book came about. I've found that since I've put these stories down on paper, I don't think about Vietnam as much and I sleep better. It's as if I can now let go. I still think about Vietnam on a daily basis, but I'm much more at peace about the whole experience. Like I've said in the book, this was all part of the plan for my life.

I only hope that all of my buddies, and the many others mentioned here, are at peace with themselves. Their names were changed for this book, but I can tell you that some of us still stay in contact with each other. They have become probation officers, treasury agents, farmers, restaurant owners, real estate agents, factory workers, and owners of small businesses. In other words, they are the Americans working along side of you every day. I am proud to call them friends.

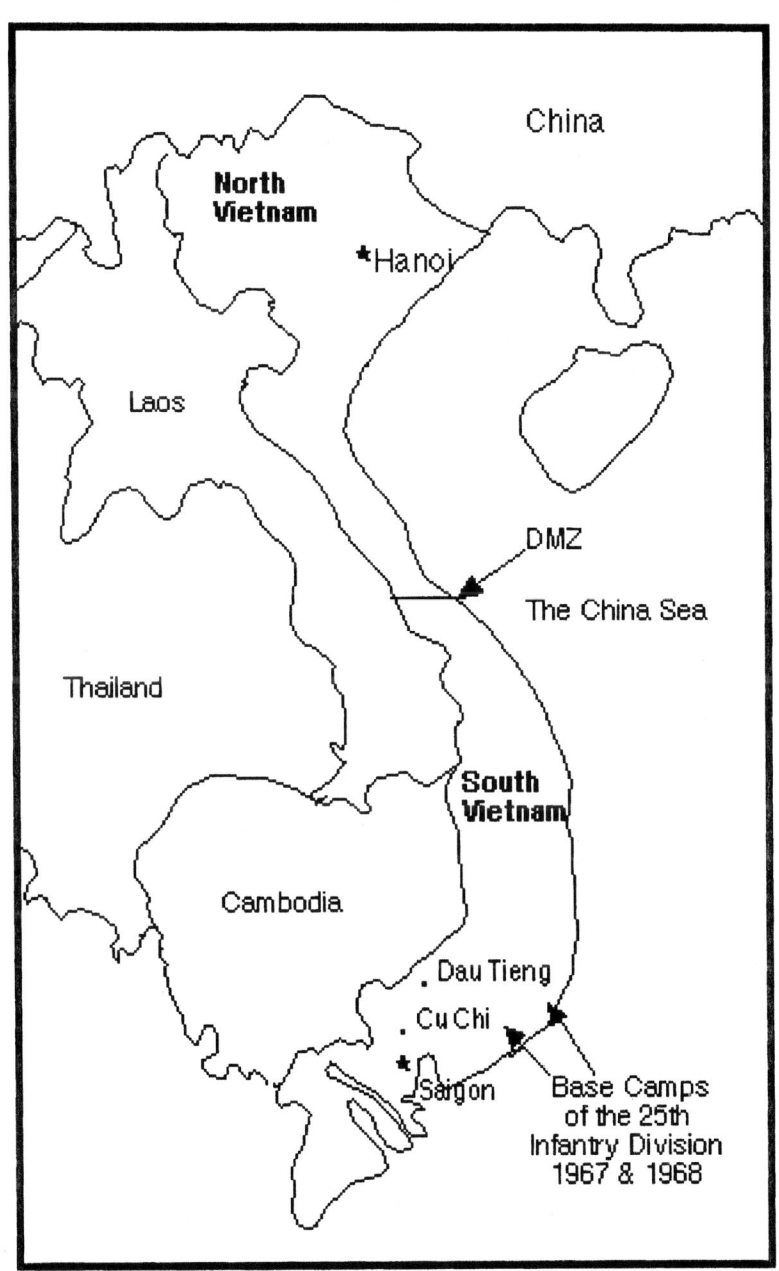

China

North Vietnam

★Hanoi

Laos

DMZ

The China Sea

Thailand

South Vietnam

Cambodia

. Dau Tieng

. Cu Chi

★Saigon

Base Camps
of the 25th
Infantry Division
1967 & 1968

215

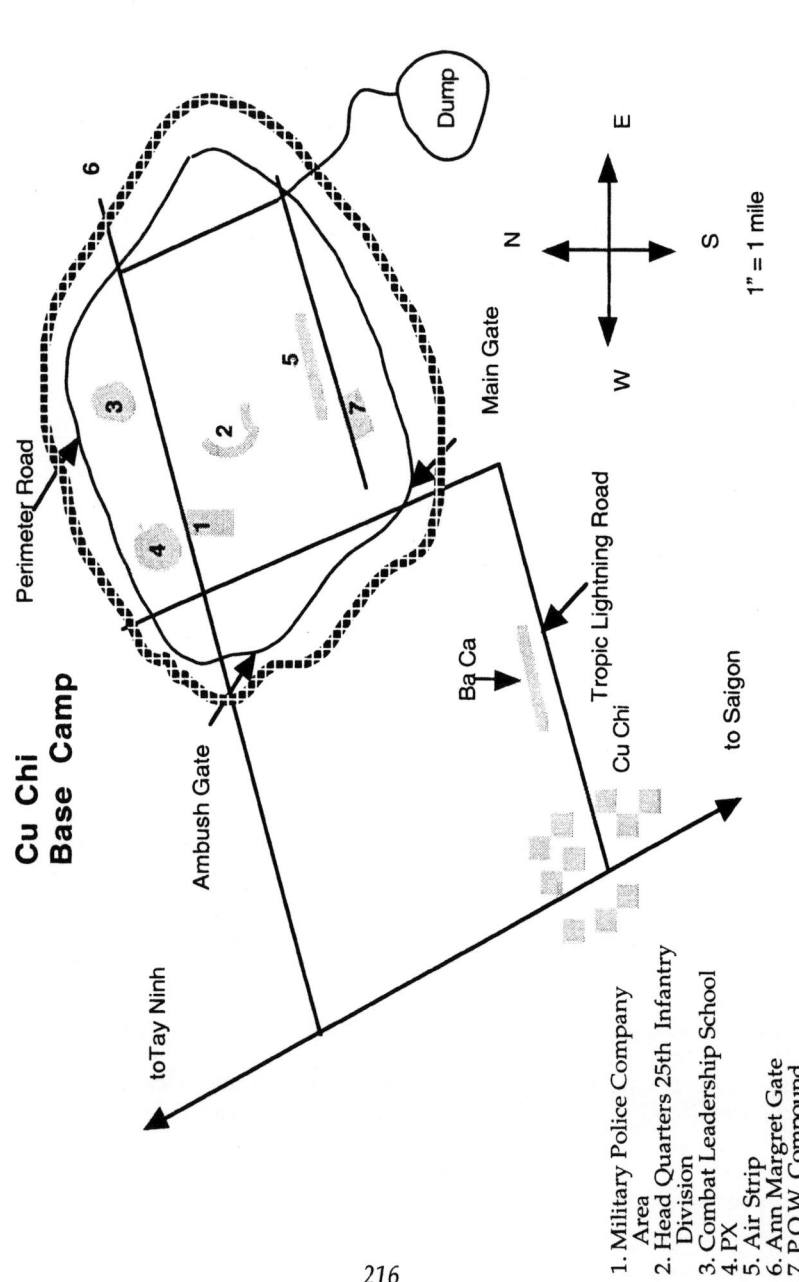

Cu Chi Base Camp

Perimeter Road

Ambush Gate

to Tay Ninh

Dump

Main Gate

Ba Ca

Cu Chi

Tropic Lightning Road

to Saigon

N   E
W   S

1" = 1 mile

1. Military Police Company Area
2. Head Quarters 25th Infantry Division
3. Combat Leadership School
4. PX
5. Air Strip
6. Ann Margret Gate
7. P.O.W. Compound

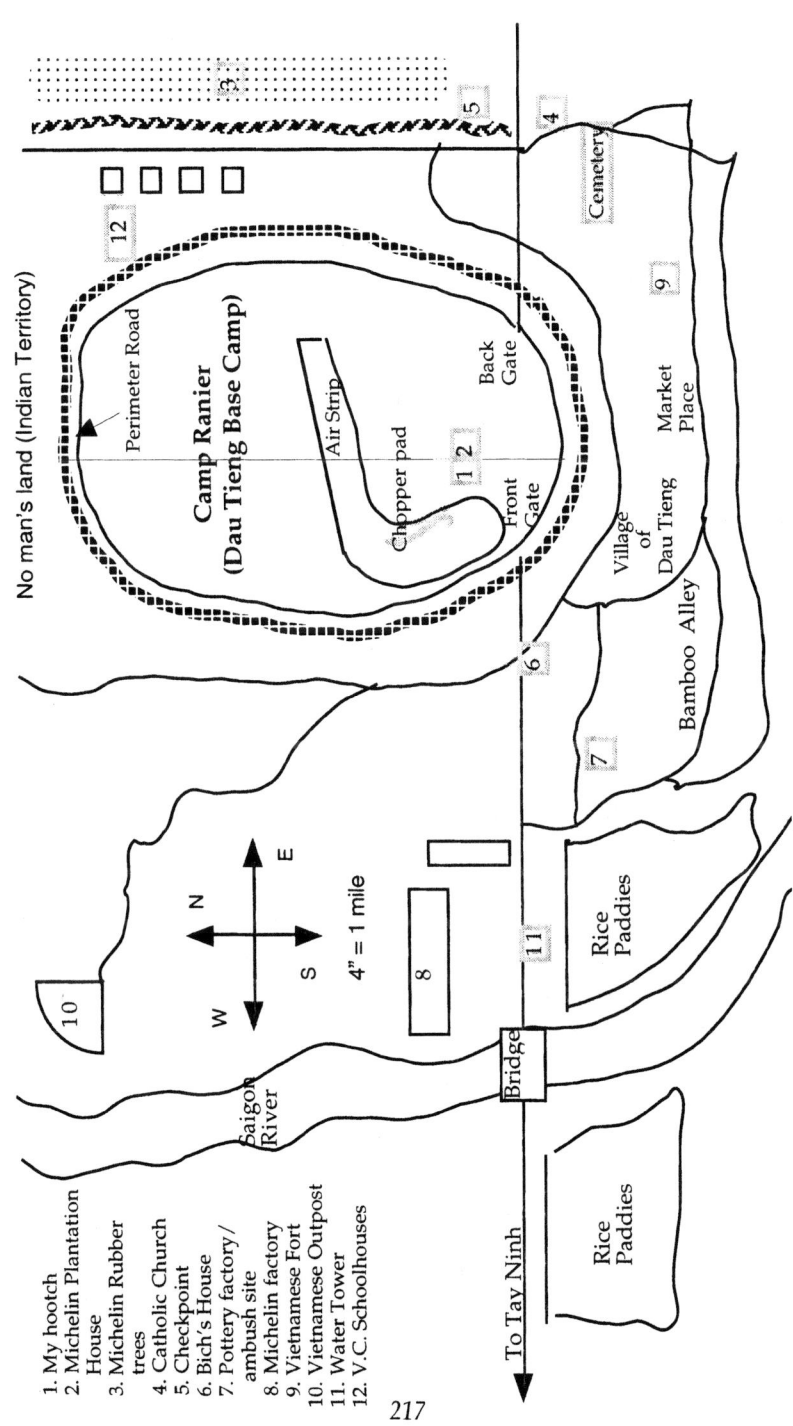

No man's land (Indian Territory)

Camp Ranier
(Dau Tieng Base Camp)

Perimeter Road

Air Strip

Chopper pad

Front Gate

Back Gate

Cemetery

Village of Dau Tieng

Market Place

Bamboo Alley

Saigon River

N
E
S
W

4" = 1 mile

Rice Paddies

Rice Paddies

Bridge

To Tay Ninh

1. My hootch
2. Michelin Plantation House
3. Michelin Rubber trees
4. Catholic Church
5. Checkpoint
6. Pottery factory/ ambush site
7. Michelin factory
8. Vietnamese Fort
9. Vietnamese Outpost
10. Water Tower
11. V.C. Schoolhouses

OFFICERS AND MEN IN THE 25th U.S INFANTRY DIVISION

There will be more shelled attacks and annihilating battles which are fearer coming to you.

Our people's liberation armed forces are revolved to defeat the U.S aggressors who are causing a mourning of our native land. Our hostility towards the U.S aggressors and Thieu-Ky dictatorial traitors and determination to use ourselves blood and bone in view to winning independence and freedom will be our strength for overcoming of the enemies.

The day when the U S bellicose ringleader band still carry out the aggressive war and cover Thieu-Ky traitors, then we look you as the enemy number one of our nation.

However, the South Vietnam people have highly honoured and grately thankful the U.S people who have sympthized and supported our struggle for peace, independence, freedom and neutrality. That mean:

-The South Vietnam National Front For Liberation strictly observes its lenient policy towards the U.S presoners of war and enable and help them to return to their family if they recognize their sins against the Vietnamese people as the case of Claude Mc. Clure RA.14.703.075, black american and George Edward Smith RA.13.522.780.

-The Front kighly welcome the U.S citizen's struggles to demand Johnson administration to stop immediately the U.S aggressive war in South Vietnam.

-The Front highly praise the courage actions of your friends to oppose to your being sent to the battlefront massacreing our peasants in the liberated area. Only so doing you can look yourselves for away out.

-The Front will arrange the repatriation of anti-war US GI's crossing over to the Front's side.

DVDXOI

Viet Cong propaganda that was collected near the Dau Tieng Base Camp.

Scotty riding Convoy Security from Cu Chi to Saigon.

The dump at Cu Chi before we gained control of it.

My .45 and Bic's live scorpion.
"Big Medicine," she said.

Charlie, our pet monkey. He's the small one.
The picture also shows the rubber trees that our
hootch was built around.

Phil, me, Gary and Lux after securing Checkpoint Three.

Damage done by an anti-tank tilt rod mine
that we almost hit with our jeep.

This huge bull frog went into the chow
at Checkpoint Three.

Our cheiu hoi.
(A Viet Cong who turned himself in)

I'm on Checkpoint Duty, with the aid of all the ARVN's
in the bunker behind me.

The Michelin Pottery Factory. It was the site
of several ambushes we set up.

This is the view from the pottery factory's wall.
Bamboo Alley is to the right of the picture.
The post is pointing right to it.

Rubber trees and the east side of the base camp perimeter.

The plantation house belonging to Michelin.
The beautiful French built mansion would eventually
be destroyed.

This picture was taken from the side door of a helicopter about to land at Dau Tieng Base Camp. At the center of the picture are the Checkpoint Three bunkers. The trees are all part of the Michelin Plantation.

My little sister, Tran Ngoc Bich, and her best friend.

Pete and Frenchie, after a day on Convoy Security.
Snowflake is on the left side of the picture and
Lifer is on the right.

This is the teacher who was cured by our "bac si".

Our homemade armored car on duty at Checkpoint Three.

The best bunker in South Vietnam.

I'm leaving a parting shot at the V.C. on the 'schoolhouse'.

Pete was a little shaky (and so was I) when he took
this picture. We had just been shot at and had
crashed into the concertina wire.

I've Passed This Way Before

GLOSSARY

ARVN	The Army of the Republic of South Vietnam, or a member of the army.
AK-47	Kalashnikov Assault rifle. A fully automatic rifle of Soviet design. The basic individual weapon of the communist forces.
Ao Dias	A traditional Vietnamese woman's dress, which is always worn with pants because the long skirt is slit all the way to the hip on either side.
B-40 rocket	A shoulder-held rocket-propelled grenade (RPG) launcher.
Ba	Married woman. Used as a title, like Mrs.
Bac-si	Doctor. Also used to refer to American army medics.
Ba Muoi Ba	A brand name of a Vietnamese beer.
Base camp	Brigade or division-size headquarters.
Chao	Hello or goodby-depending on the context.
Charlie	Viet Cong.
Chinook	A large, twin-rotor helicopter used primarily for carrying cargo or large numbers of soldiers on non tactical movements.
Chieu Hoi	The "open arms" amnesty program to encourage surrender by VC and NVA soldiers and cadres. Around 200,000 came over to the south Vietnamese side.

Clay more mine	An American anti-personnel mine which was set up above ground and was aimed so that detonation would send out a blast of hundreds of steel balls in the desired direction. The name was taken from the name of the huge Scottish broad sword which was also used to cut a swath through enemy ranks.
Click	Slang term for a kilometer
Connex Container	Corrugated metal packing crate, approximately six feet in length.
Contact	Firing on or being fired upon by the enemy.
Civilian Irregular Defense Group	American-financed irregular military units which were led by members of Special Forces A-teams. Members of these units were Vietnamese nationals, but were usually members of ethnic minorities in the country.
Co	Unmarried woman. Used as a title, like Miss.
C-ration	The combat ration issued to American soldiers. Each ration consisted of a can of some basic course, a can of fruit, a packet of some type of dessert, a packet of powdered cocoa, a small pack of cigarettes, and two pieces of chewing gum.
Di	Go.
Di di mau!	Get the hell outta here! Literally, "Go go quickly."
Dust-off	An emergency medical evacuation by helicopter.

Flack vest	An armored vest issued to American soldiers. They were hot, heavy, and often not worn despite the protection they offered.
Free-fire zone	An area, cleared of civilians, within which artillery and aircraft could fire without having to obtain clearance. Any persons found within a free-fire zone were presumed to be enemy.
Hat-up	Direction to put your helmets on and prepare to move out.
Hootch	A simply constructed dwelling, either military or civilian.
In-country	On the ground in Vietnam.
KIA	Killed in action.
Lambretta	A three wheeled, open air mini-bus powered by a motorcycle engine.
Landing zone	A designated area for the landing of helicopters and the off-loading of men and cargo.
LP	(1) Listening post; forward observation post of two or three men; (2) Amphibious landing platform; used by infantry for storming beaches from the sea.
LZ	Landing Zone.
M-16	The standard issue, fully automatic assault rifle used by the South Vietnamese and American forces.

M-79	A grenade launcher. A shoulder-fired weapon resembling a sawed-off, hugely bored shotgun; It could lob its projectiles more than a hundred meters.
N.V.A.	North Vietnamese Army
Nung	Tribes people of Chinese origin from the highlands of North Vietnam; some who moved south worked with U.S. Special Forces.
Poncho liner	Nylon insert to the military rain poncho, used as a blanket.
Quad fifty	Four .50 caliber machine guns fired by one soldier in a revolving turret mounted on a truck.
R.P.G.	Rocket propelled grenade.
Sampan	A Vietnamese peasant's boat.
Sapper	A VC or NVA commando, usually armed with explosives.
Short-Timer	Soldier nearing the end of his tour in Vietnam.
Starlight Scope	A night observation device that uses reflected light from the stars and moon. It intensifies light and allows you to see into the night through a binocular type of device. Looking through a starlight, the entire scene is green, but you can see.
Steel pot	Helmet.
V.C.	Viet Cong.

Viet Cong	The Communist-led forces fighting the South Vietnamese government. (Cong is short for Cong-san, which means "Communist.") The political wing was known as the National Liberation Front, and the military was called the Peoples Liberation Armed Forces. Both the NLF and PLAF were directed by the People's Revolutionary Party (PRP), the southern branch of the Vietnamese Communist Party, which received direction from Hanoi through COSVN, which was located in III Corps on the Cambodian border. After 1968, as negotiations began in Paris, the NLF established the Provisional Revolutionary Government to appear politically legitimate.
WIA	Wounded in action.
The World	The G.I.s' term for the United States.

To order additional copies of *I've **Passed This Way Before***, complete the information below.

Ship to: (please print)

Name_____

Address_____

City, State, Zip_____

Day phone_____

_____copies of *I've Passed This Way Before* @ \$11.95 each \$_____

Postage and handling @ \$3.95 per book   \$_____

Total   \$_____

Make checks payable to **Mike Coney**

Send to: Mike Coney

15965 Fendt Farm Drive - Holland, MI 49424

- -

To order additional copies of *I've **Passed This Way Before***, complete the information below.

Ship to: (please print)

Name_____

Address_____

City, State, Zip_____

Day phone_____

_____copies of *I've Passed This Way Before* @ \$11.95 each \$_____

Postage and handling @ \$3.95 per book   \$_____

Total   \$_____

Make checks payable to **Mike Coney**

Send to: Mike Coney

15965 Fendt Farm Drive - Holland, MI 49424